Presented to

_____

By

_____

On the Occasion of

_____

Date

All Scripture quotations, unless otherwise noted, are taken from the King James Version of the Bible.

Scripture quotations marked NKJV are taken from the New King James Version. Copyright © 1979, 1980, 1982 by Thomas Nelson, Inc. Used by permission. All rights reserved.

Scripture quotations marked ASV are taken from the American Standard Version of the Bible.

Scripture quotations marked NIV are taken from the HOLY BIBLE, NEW INTERNATIONAL VERSION®. NIV®. Copyright © 1973, 1978, 1984 by International Bible Society. Used by permission of Zondervan Publishing House. All rights reserved.

Scripture quotations marked NLT are taken from the *Holy Bible*, New Living Translation, copyright © 1996. Used by permission of Tyndale House Publishers, Inc. Wheaton, Illinois 60189, U.S.A. All rights reserved.

Cover art © Comstock

Published by Barbour Publishing, Inc., P.O. Box 719, Uhrichsville, Ohio 44683, www.barbourbooks.com

Our mission is to publish and distribute inspirational products offering exceptional value and biblical encouragement to the masses.

Member of the
Evangelical Christian
Publishers Association

Printed in the United States of America.
5

THE
WONDER OF
CHRISTMAS

*50 Meditations
on the Birth
of Christ*

DANIEL PARTNER

BARBOUR
PUBLISHING

For Radina and Donn Welton—
with gratitude

But as touching brotherly love
ye need not that I write unto you.
1 THESSALONIANS 4:9

INTRODUCTION

Sometimes I wonder about Christmas. What is it really all about? People shop, wrap, and give gifts; cook, serve, and eat food; go to parties, send Christmas cards, and drive around to see lights; attend movies, plays, and musical productions; and visit friends and family in spite of the stresses of traveling. Then, abruptly, after the Christmas morning cleanup, it's all over until the next year.

"Christmas is about the birth of Jesus Christ," you may say. But I've heard others say that Christmas is for children. . .that it is a time for families to gather. . .or an occasion to help the needy. And of course merchants see it as a vital time for sales. On the "spiritual" level, some churches are crowded on Christmas Eve—but I've attended such services where Christ is hardly mentioned except in the old standard hymns of the season and the Gospel reading from Luke.

I think that the vital understanding of the birth of Christ has been buried by *Christmas.* So I've written this book for anyone who desires to pause each day of this hectic season and truly remember the wonder of Christmas—Jesus Christ himself.

Here are twenty-five days of readings, drawn from Scripture, about the first coming of the Lord. Each day has a morning and an evening reading whose topics are related to the same set of verses. Some of these verses are ones you would expect to read in such a book—the familiar stories of Mary and Joseph, wise men, and shepherds. You may be surprised to see some verses from Paul's epistles, the Old Testament prophets, or the Book of Revelation. Even so, they all shed light on the meaning of the birth of Jesus Christ.

I hope that this book will ignite in you a fresh revelation of Christ—that it will cause you to say, like those ancient shepherds, "Let's go to Bethlehem and see this thing that has happened, which the Lord has told us about" (Luke 2:15 NIV).

DANIEL PARTNER
Coos Bay, Oregon
June 2003

DECEMBER 1

And so it was, that, while they were there,
the days were accomplished that she should be delivered.
And she brought forth her firstborn son, and wrapped him
in swaddling clothes, and laid him in a manger;
because there was no room for them in the inn.

LUKE 2:6–7

MORNING

While driving on U.S. Route 3 through New Hampshire's north country toward Quebec, you enter the northern-most town in the state—Pittsburg. There in someone's dooryard is a small shed of weathered wood with an open front covered with chicken wire. Its year-round occupants are plastic figures of a man and a woman who are kneeling by a manger. These three-quarter-sized figures make up a Christmas nativity scene. Year-round, hunters and fishers, loggers and truckers, natives and tourists pass by this display. It is most visible on long summer days when no colored lights surround the shed. The bright sun and green grass make it an eye-catching reminder of the birth of Jesus Christ.

Theologians call Christ's birth the *Incarnation*. The Gospel of John describes it like this: "The Word was made flesh, and dwelt among us" (John 1:14).

The famous poet, Ben Jonson (1572–1637), wrote of it in "A Hymn of the Nativity of My Savior":

I sing the birth, was born tonight,
The author both of life and light. . .

Our children sing, "Away in a manger, no crib for a bed," and a citizen of Pittsburg, New Hampshire, uses old planks, colored plastic, and chicken wire to tell of the birth of a child who was God. But from the simplest to the most sublime, nothing we can do or say or sing can adequately represent this event. *The Creator became a creature!* Crude chicken wire and well-crafted phrases are equally impotent to explain this. *The living God lives a human life!* Use plastic, use poetry—try as you might, nothing will do to completely describe it. Combine the voices of apostles, poets, theologians, and every choir of children on earth to sing the significance of the God-man. Yet silence works just about as well.

Construct a cathedral, cobble together a

REMEMBER EACH DAY
THE WONDER OF
CHRIST'S BIRTH.

crèche, or create a holiday called Christmas—whatever you do, remember *each day* the wonder of Christ's birth and pray, "Dear heavenly Father, thank you for sending your Son into this world."

NIGHT

Whatever became of the inn—the one whose keeper could not receive Mary and Joseph on the eve of Jesus' birth?

Some ancient man built that inn of stone or bricks of clay. Perhaps this builder mixed and spread stucco across its walls for a smooth appearance, then hung shutters to cover its windows, tamped down the dirt floor, firm and level, and attached a gate or door.

A man and a woman had made that inn their home, prepared food and drink, and took in guests. Was it the only inn in Bethlehem? If so, then its proprietors were surely well known in town. Perhaps he was prominent in the synagogue, and she was sought out by other women at the town's well. This couple may well have had children and grandchildren of their own. Could they have been pleased to turn away the man from Nazareth with his pregnant wife?

Then, after Mary's child had been born in one of the inn's outbuildings and Herod's soldiers came to kill all the little boys in town (Matthew 2:16), whom did the innkeepers lose to this slaughter? Grandsons, sons, nephews, and cousins all fell beneath the Roman blades. Sobs of grief must have echoed throughout that inn as family blood stained its floor.

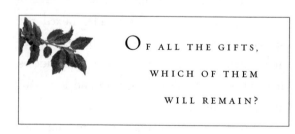

OF ALL THE GIFTS,
WHICH OF THEM
WILL REMAIN?

So whatever became of that inn? It is gone; it is dust. Not only is the inn dust, the innkeepers have returned to dust along with all the jars in their kitchen and guests in their rooms. Only one artifact remains to memorialize their existence—the record of the birth of the Christ-child.

Maybe the story of the too-full inn is a parable for us in the season of Christmas: Of all the gifts and gatherings that fill your heart this month, which of them will remain when you have returned to dust? Only Jesus Christ really matters.

DECEMBER 2

And in the sixth month the angel Gabriel was sent

from God unto a city of Galilee, named Nazareth,

to a virgin espoused to a man whose name was Joseph,

of the house of David; and the virgin's name was Mary.

And the angel came in unto her, and said,

Hail, thou that art highly favoured, the Lord is with thee:

blessed art thou among women.

LUKE 1:26–28

MORNING

The Christmas story begins with the amazing visit of God's archangel to a young woman. In his poem "Mary and Gabriel," the English poet Rupert Brooke (1887–1915) described the appearing of Gabriel to Mary in this way:

> Young Mary, loitering once her garden way,
> Felt a warm splendour grow in the April day,
> As wine that blushes water through.
> And soon,
> Out of the gold air of the afternoon,

One knelt before her: hair he had of fire,
Bound back above his ears with golden wire,
Baring the eager marble of his face.

Imagine the torrent of feelings that must have surged through Mary's heart at that moment. Then the angel spoke! "Fear not, Mary: for thou hast found favour with God. And, behold, thou shalt conceive in thy womb, and bring forth a son, and shalt call his name JESUS. He shall be great, and shall be called the Son of the Highest: and the Lord God shall give unto him the throne of his father David: and he shall reign over the house of Jacob for ever; and of his kingdom there shall be no end" (Luke 1:30–33). These words weren't spoken to a prophet, a leader, or an elder. Rather, this good news was to a young woman for whom childhood was still a fresh memory.

It is Mary, an extraordinary personality, upon whom the light of the Christmas story first falls. Unfortunately, too many Protestant Christians fail to appreciate Mary—in part because the Roman Catholic Church gave her the title "The Queen of Heaven" and allows her to be venerated as the mother of God. This caused a reaction among Protestant believers that transferred Mary to the second-class coach of the gospel train.

God didn't give Mary divinity. Instead, something much more significant occurred. God used Mary's obedience to give Christ his humanity! 1 Timothy 3:16 says that this is the mystery of godliness, that Jesus Christ is entirely God and thoroughly man. Where did he obtain this humanity? It didn't come miraculously through a snap of God's fingers but through this young woman's pregnancy and pain of labor.

GOD USED MARY'S OBEDIENCE TO GIVE CHRIST HIS HUMANITY!

Mary's response to Gabriel foretells her important place in the gospel story: "Oh, how I praise the Lord. How I rejoice in God my Savior! For he took notice of his lowly servant girl, and now generation after generation will call me blessed" (Luke 1:46–48 NLT).

NIGHT

Gabriel was very busy in the beginning of the Gospel of Luke. The angel appeared to two people and received from them two very different responses. The first appearance was to old Zechariah (Luke 1:11–20) and the other to young Mary (Luke 1:26–28).

When the angel told Zechariah that his elderly wife was to have a son, he responded, "How can I be sure of this? I am an old man and my wife is well along in years" (Luke 1:18 NIV). Zechariah couldn't accept the Lord's words and so asked for a sign to prove them true. Luke 1:19–20 shows that this was unbelief.

When Gabriel told Mary that she would have a child, she wondered, "But how can this happen? I am a virgin." The angel informed her of what God would do: "The Holy Ghost shall come upon thee, and the power of the Highest shall overshadow thee: therefore also that holy thing which shall be born of thee shall be called the Son of God" (Luke 1:35). Mary's response to Gabriel made her the first New Testament believer. She said, "Behold the handmaid of the Lord; be it unto me according to thy word" (Luke 1:38). This response came out of faith, the faith that can verify the unseen things of God (Hebrews 11:1). So Mary was one of those "who through faith and patience inherit the promises" (Hebrews 6:12).

This is the way Rupert Brooke ended his poem about the appearance of Gabriel to Mary:

> The great wings were spread
> Showering glory on the fields, and fire.
> The whole air, singing, bore him up,
>   and higher,
> Unswerving, unreluctant. Soon he shone

A gold speck in the gold skies; then was gone.
The air was colder, and gray. She stood alone.

 REMEMBER THE
WOMAN WHO GAVE
BELIEVERS THEIR
FIRST EXAMPLE OF FAITH.

The responses of Mary and Zechariah to the good news are good guides to us today. As you pass this Christmas season, remember the woman who gave the Son of God his humanity and his believers their first example of faith.

DECEMBER 3

And Mary said, My soul doth magnify the Lord,
and my spirit hath rejoiced in God my Saviour.
For he hath regarded the low estate of his handmaiden:
for, behold, from henceforth all generations shall call me
blessed. For he that is mighty hath done to me
great things; and holy is his name. And his mercy is
on them that fear him from generation to generation.
He hath shewed strength with his arm; he hath scattered
the proud in the imagination of their hearts. He hath put
down the mighty from their seats, and exalted them of low
degree. He hath filled the hungry with good things; and
the rich he hath sent empty away. He hath holpen his
servant Israel, in remembrance of his mercy; as he spake
to our fathers, to Abraham, and to his seed for ever.

LUKE 1:46–55

MORNING

The angel Gabriel appeared to young Mary. Just imagine it. She heard the potent words that God would, through her, be born as a man—the Savior of the world! Not surprisingly, at first Mary "was greatly troubled at his words" (Luke 1:29 NIV). Whom would this not overwhelm?

Soon Mary hurried to Zechariah's home in the hill country of Judea to visit her cousin Elizabeth, Zechariah's wife. Certainly as she traveled, Mary considered what had happened and repeated the angel's words over and over in her mind. At some point on this journey, the significance of it all dawned on her. As she arrived and entered the house, Elizabeth greeted her and Mary exclaimed, "My soul doth magnify the Lord, and my spirit hath rejoiced in God my Saviour!" (Luke 1:46–47). She continued on in a rich soliloquy about God's purpose in the birth of Christ. This portion of Scripture (Luke 1:46–55) is called "Mary's Song" or the "Magnificat" after the first word of the Latin translation.

Mary had pondered the words of God, spoken to her by an angel. Consider the effect this had upon her. Before, she was merely "a virgin espoused to a man whose name was Joseph" (Luke 1:27). Scholars say that she was probably just in her early teens. If so, she must have been rather meek. But suddenly, she is bold and proclaiming without hesitation, "My soul doth magnify the Lord, and my spirit hath rejoiced in God my Saviour!" Surely she had been unsure of herself as the betrothed of an older man, but no more. "Behold, from henceforth all generations shall call me blessed," she says, and Mary's confidence overflows as she proclaims, "He that is mighty hath done to me great things; and holy is his name."

The girl has been transformed into a prophet on par with the greatest of the Old Testament. In God's name, she condemns the proud and wealthy, has compassion on the poor, and invokes the name of the illustrious Abraham. This is the effect that the Word of God can have on any soul—even yours.

THIS IS THE EFFECT THAT THE WORD OF GOD CAN HAVE ON ANY SOUL— EVEN YOURS.

Gabriel gave Mary only about 150 words to ponder. You and I have the entire Bible to consider! Not only so, "Long ago God spoke many times and in many ways to our ancestors through the prophets. But now in these final days, *he has spoken to us through his Son*" (Hebrews 1:1–2 NLT emphasis added).

NIGHT

You'd think that Mary would have been a little tired after the journey to her cousin's house in the hills. Instead, she was invigorated and filled with the Spirit because of the words of God that she heard from Gabriel. With great energy and passion, Mary spoke of God's ways.

We, too, can be invigorated with the joy of the meaning of Christmas. Yet, most everyone complains of feeling exhausted by the Christmas season. The level of activity can wear down the body and financial expenditure can drain the bank account. "Mary's Song" explains the actual reason we have such experiences at this time of year: "He hath scattered the proud in the imagination of their hearts" (Luke 1:51). We suppose that we can find true satisfaction in the excess of Christmas gifts and food and gatherings. So we are scattered, weakened in the imagination of our hearts.

Now don't get me wrong. I'm not like those Puritans of old who attempted to ban the observance of Christmas. I like it when the cheerful holiday lights appear in the darkness of winter; I'm happy to be invited to a gathering of friends where I can indulge in some special foods; and there's nothing like getting a gift from someone who loves me. But, I have to be careful that my imagination doesn't run away with me. I've been scattered too many times in the fantasy that I can really find satisfaction in such things.

Mary sings, "He hath filled the hungry with good things; and the rich he hath sent empty away" (Luke 1:53). When you are exhausted in various ways by the Christmas season, ask yourself this question, "Have I been filled with good things, or is God sending me away empty?"

Again, I am not proposing that anyone cease

the celebration of Christmas. I only hope that Christians will personally add to it the remembrance of God's mercy. Daily in the hustle and bustle of the season, in the grocery store, at the mall, in sending greeting cards, and gathering gifts, please consider the thing that occupied and energized Mary as she traveled to Elizabeth's—she would be with child and give birth to a son, and give him the name Jesus! And, "He will be very great and will be called the Son of the Most High. And the Lord God will give him the throne of his ancestor David. And he will reign over Israel forever; his Kingdom will never end" (Luke 1:32–33 NLT). See if this fills you with the truly good things of Christmas!

CONSIDER THE THING
THAT OCCUPIED AND
ENERGIZED MARY.

DECEMBER 4

When they had heard the king, they departed;
and, lo, the star, which they saw in the east,
went before them, till it came and stood over
where the young child was. When they saw the star,
they rejoiced with exceeding great joy.
And when they were come into the house, they saw the
young child with Mary his mother, and fell down,
and worshipped him: and when they had opened
their treasures, they presented unto him gifts;
gold, and frankincense and myrrh.

MATTHEW 2:9–11

MORNING

The English poet Christina Rossetti (1830–1894) wrote the lyrics to a most beautiful and meaningful Advent hymn. It begins:

> In the bleak midwinter, frosty wind
> made moan,
> Earth stood hard as iron, water like a stone;
> Snow had fallen, snow on snow, snow
> on snow,
> In the bleak midwinter, long ago.

The poet imagines the conditions surrounding Christ's birth. It is a gray, cold, midwinter day. Outside, the wind moans, the earth is as hard as iron, the frozen waters like stone, and everywhere is "snow on snow, snow on snow." This is a poem, so it does not pretend to describe the actual weather conditions in Bethlehem at the time Jesus was born. But it does truthfully portray the human state and the condition of our souls without Jesus. These four lines tell of the earth's desperate need for the warm love of a Savior.

Rossetti uses the next stanzas of the poem to beautifully express how out of place our Savior was in this setting. She observes that heaven cannot hold God nor can earth sustain him, yet in the bleak midwinter, a stable sufficed as the birthplace of God incarnate—Jesus Christ.

In the end Christina Rossetti tells of the earnest impulse of those who realize who Jesus is:

What can I give him, poor as I am?
If I were a shepherd, I would bring a lamb;
If I were a Wise Man, I would do my part;
Yet what can I give him? Give him my heart.

Her gift, like the birth of God as a man, is entirely out of the ordinary, yet absolutely necessary. The shepherd's gift of a lamb and the magi's precious gifts were useful at the time, no doubt. But do you really possess anything that God could ever *need?* Yet, you do have the one thing that he *wants.*

THE THING THAT
GOD REALLY DESIRES—
YOUR HEART.

This is the season of gift buying, gift wrapping, and gift giving. As you witness the many presents passing from hand to hand, pause and ask yourself the poet's question, "What can I give to God, poor as I am?" The gifts you may give to God, your money or your time, merely point toward the thing that God really desires—your heart.

NIGHT

We know the wise men presented wonderful gifts to Jesus, but I wonder if they knew the significance their gifts held.

Henry Wadsworth Longfellow (1807–1882) wrote a poem about these magi titled "The Three Kings." Concerning their gifts, he wrote:

They laid their offerings at his feet:
The gold was their tribute to a King,
The frankincense, with its odor sweet,
Was for the Priest, the Paraclete,
The myrrh for the body's burying.

Doubtless, the myrrh indicates the redeeming death of Christ. Myrrh was commonly used when preparing a body for burial. Nicodemus used roughly seventy-five pounds of embalming ointment made from myrrh and aloes when he buried Jesus (John 19:39). Myrrh is plant resin and is harvested by cutting through the bark of a tree. This cutting is evocative of the Lord's experience on the cross when a soldier pierced his side (John 19:34).

The frankincense is symbolic of Christ's priesthood since the priests of Israel offered incense in worship and the offering of the sacrifices. "He is the kind of high priest we need," Scripture declares, "because he is holy and blameless" (Hebrews 7:26 NLT). Since frankincense, like myrrh, is a plant resin, it, too, indicates Christ's sacrificial death. Longfellow says that frankincense also symbolizes the Paraclete. This is the Holy Spirit as the Comforter who, like a fragrance, brings Christ to our remembrance (John 14:26).

Gold is a gift for a king, true enough. But it also indicates that this little boy, whom the magi came to worship, was God. Gold is often used in Scripture as a symbol for God such as in Job

22:23–25 (NIV), which says, "If you return to the Almighty, you will be restored. . .then the Almighty will be your gold, the choicest silver for you." The fact that gold does not corrode shows God's purity and incorruptibility. It is also the most malleable and ductile of all metals—one ounce of gold can be beaten into a three-hundred-square-foot sheet of foil. This is suggestive of God's flexibility as he is patient and forgiving of us.

GOLD, FRANKINCENSE, AND MYRRH REVEAL JUST WHO WAS LIVING THERE.

Gold, frankincense, and myrrh. These three precious gifts brought by magi to an obscure Middle Eastern place reveal just who was living there—it was the redeeming Savior and High Priest who was the very God of the universe!

DECEMBER 5

Now when Jesus was born in Bethlehem of Judaea

in the days of Herod the king, behold,

there came wise men from the east to Jerusalem, saying,

Where is he that is born King of the Jews?

for we have seen his star in the east,

and are come to worship him.

MATTHEW 2:1–2

MORNING

Henry
Wadsworth Longfellow was an American poet
and linguist. He is best known as the author of
"Paul Revere's Ride" and "The Song of Hiawatha."
Several of his lesser-known works were written on
Christian subjects.

His poem "The Three Kings," quoted in
yesterday's reading, romanticizes the original
story of the wise men as found in Matthew
2:1–12. Beginning with its title, the poem puts
across many modern-day misconceptions about
these men, like the idea that there were three of

them. Its first three stanzas describe the wise men as richly dressed and traveling at night by starlight. But the Bible does not give us this much detail about them. No one knows who these men were, where exactly they came from, or how many of them made the journey.

THOSE WHO SHOULD
HAVE WELCOMED
THE MESSIAH
MISSED THEIR OPPORTUNITY.

The star they followed is an equal mystery. It led them as far as Jerusalem, where the travelers seem to have lost sight of it. So they went to King Herod and asked him, "Where is he that is born King of the Jews?" (Matthew 2:2). Herod had no idea what to tell them, so he called in the priests and religious teachers of Jerusalem. They knew exactly where Christ was to be born, referring to Micah 5:2, saying, "And thou Bethlehem, in the land of Juda, art not the least among the princes of Juda: for out of thee shall come a Governor, that shall rule my people Israel" (Matthew 2:6).

These religious men knew that these strangers had come to find the long-awaited Messiah. I wonder, though: If there was a possibility that the Christ could be found at that moment in nearby Bethlehem, why didn't they go with the travelers and seek him out? Instead, they did nothing. Although this story is baffling, this much is known: Those who should have welcomed the Messiah missed their opportunity, while foreigners traveled far to honor the king of the Jews.

That was long ago. Today, church and culture have combined to create an entire season of the year in which Jesus Christ is supposed to be honored. But if some dusty strangers arrived at your holiday party wishing to find the Christ, where would you direct their search, and would you go along with them in hope of finding the Lord?

NIGHT

The wise men lived at the time of the Lord's first appearing, yet their story tells something about the Second Coming. Two lessons emerge from the magi's encounter with the religious leaders in Jerusalem.

First, these priests and scribes knew the verse well that tells where the Messiah would appear, yet they didn't go to Bethlehem to find him. This shows that Bible knowledge alone will never secure our preparedness to meet the Lord. Yes, it is good to know the prophecies and promises of Scripture about the Lord. However, it is better to love the Lord. Such love causes a sincere longing to see him face-to-face. Remember, a crown of righteousness is promised to all those who love his appearing (2 Timothy 4:7–8).

No servant can serve two masters.

The second lesson we learn from the magi's encounter with the religious leaders of Jerusalem is that faith and politics do not mix well. Something Jesus said in a later context explains this, "No servant can serve two masters: for either he will hate the one, and love the other; or else he will hold to the one, and despise the other" (Luke 16:13).

These religious leaders were in collusion with Herod, the political power of the day. To go to Bethlehem, they would have had to leave behind their earthly master, Herod, in order to find the heavenly One. This was risky and they decided they had too much to lose in the way of comfort, prestige, and power, so they stayed home.

After their visit to Bethlehem, the wise men didn't return to tell Herod where to find Jesus (Matthew 2:12). Instead, they obeyed their heavenly Master who warned them in a dream not to return to Herod as he had asked. Because of the wise men's obedience to God, the young Christ escaped the fury of Herod who, hoping to slay his rival, sent soldiers to kill all the boys in and around Bethlehem who were two years old and under (Matthew 2:16).

I think that certain church leaders today should learn this lesson from Herod's religious leaders, who chose to serve their earthly master over the heavenly Master. If they would transfer their hope from American politics to the appearing of Christ, the world would greatly benefit. And they, like Paul, could boast, "I have kept the faith: Henceforth there is laid up for me a crown of righteousness, which the Lord, the righteous judge, shall give me at that day: and not to me only, but unto all them also that love his appearing" (2 Timothy 4:7–8).

DECEMBER 6

In the beginning was the Word,
and the Word was with God,
and the Word was God. . . .
And the Word was made flesh,
and dwelt among us, (and we beheld his glory,
the glory as of the only begotten of the Father,)
full of grace and truth.

JOHN 1:1, 14

MORNING

When I was a little boy and appeared in my Sunday school's Christmas pageant, I played a shepherd. This role was given to all children who were too young to play the glamorous characters like Mary, Joseph, angels, and wise men. There must have been at least a dozen of us traipsing and tripping down the aisle of the church that night. I remember that my turban was an actual bath towel and my robe was the same bed sheet that had formerly transformed me into a ghost on Halloween.

No doubt the script of our Christmas pageant

was based on the stories told in the Gospels of Matthew and Luke. These accounts tell of the *action* surrounding the birth of Jesus Christ. But the Gospel of John cuts through these descriptive accounts and simply tells the *significance* of what happened. John's account provides no opportunity to fall into sentimentality or nostalgia about Christmas. Neither does it lend itself well to pageants on Christmas Eve.

THE WORD,

WHO WAS GOD,

WAS MADE FLESH.

Here is what John tells us: *The Word, who was God, was made flesh.* This means not only that Jesus was really and truly a man, but also that he subjected himself to the miseries and calamities of the human nature. *God became flesh!*

The Bible has much to say about the flesh and the significance of Christ becoming flesh. Flesh is humanity at its weakest, so Christ was crucified through weakness (2 Corinthians 13:4). Flesh is mortal and dying humanity, "a wind that passeth away, and cometh not again" (Psalm 78:39). Thus Christ was put to death in the flesh (1 Peter 3:18). Flesh is humanity tainted with sin (Colossians 2:13), so the perfectly holy Jesus Christ appeared in the likeness of sinful flesh (Romans 8:3) and was made sin for us (2 Corinthians 5:21). The man we celebrate this Christmas season was, by his birth, perfectly enabled to condemn sin in the flesh (Romans 8:3), and the wonder of Christmas is that he chose to become flesh in order to submit to death and save us from our sin.

"All flesh is grass!" cried Isaiah (Isaiah 40:6). This metaphor makes the Redeemer's love all the more wonderful. To redeem us, he was made such fleeting flesh, yet he was still the Word that was with God, the Word that came to save us. Thus, we have hope: Though the grass withers and the flower fades, "the word of our God shall stand for ever" (Isaiah 40:8).

NIGHT

This is the wonder of Christmas, that the eternal Word was made flesh and dwelt among us. He took upon himself human nature and lived in the same world as we do, under the same conditions. He had lived in glory among angels yet came to earth to live with us.

> "Sing and rejoice, O daughter of
> Zion! For behold, I am coming and
> I will dwell in your midst," says the
> LORD. "Many nations shall be joined
> to the LORD in that day, and they

shall become My people. And I will
dwell in your midst. Then you will
know that the LORD of hosts has sent
Me to you."

ZECHARIAH 2:10–11 NKJV

The Bible says that the Word "dwelt among
us." These words literally mean that he *tabernacled*
among us. Since a tabernacle is a tent, this reminds
us that he lived in low circumstances, like the common man, here on earth. Much like shepherds car-
ing for their sheep live in tents, so did the Good
Shepherd (John 10:11). Soldiers in the field also
live in tents, and when Christ was born, he, too,
took to the battlefield, set up his standard, and
pitched his tent—a human body in which he suc-
cessfully fought a war against the devil (Luke
4:1–14). When Christ lived among us, he took the
way of the patriarchs who by faith lived in the land
of promise like it was a foreign country, dwelling in
tents and confessing that they were strangers and
pilgrims on the earth (Hebrews 11:9, 13).

Of even more significance is the fact that in
ancient days, God dwelt in an elaborate tent, the

tabernacle, built by Moses (Exodus 29:42–43). Today God lives in the tent named Jesus Christ. In the days of Moses, the high priest went into the tabernacle to meet with God. Today we encounter God through Christ. Not only so, God, who spoke to Israel from the tabernacle, "has in these last days spoken to us by his Son" (Hebrews 1:2 NKJV).

THE ETERNAL WORD

DWELT AMONG US.

The Incarnation of God in Christ is beyond explanation, but images such as these help us to understand it a little. Here is one final, glorious picture: The tabernacle was the storehouse of the two tablets upon which was written God's law—the law that was impossible to keep (Romans 8:3). In contrast, John tells us the good news that the tent named Jesus Christ is full of grace and truth (John 1:14), which he freely gives to all who believe.

DECEMBER 7

And when they were departed, behold, the angel of the Lord appeareth to Joseph in a dream, saying, Arise, and take the young child and his mother, and flee into Egypt, and be thou there until I bring thee word: for Herod will seek the young child to destroy him. . . . Then Herod, when he saw that he was mocked of the wise men, was exceeding wroth, and sent forth, and slew all the children that were in Bethlehem, and in all the coasts thereof, from two years old and under, according to the time which he had diligently enquired of the wise men. Then was fulfilled that which was spoken by Jeremy the prophet, saying, In Rama was there a voice heard, lamentation, and weeping, and great mourning, Rachel weeping for her children, and would not be comforted, because they are not.

MATTHEW 2:13, 16–18

MORNING

At the time of Jesus' birth, who knew that the promised Savior had been born? Mary, Joseph, Elizabeth, and some shepherds were probably the only ones. Herod the Great got the news that a king had been born in his realm through strangers from the East—the wise men. Though it was hardly more than hearsay, Herod took the news seriously. He feared any political rival, even a newborn baby. Out of this fear came the infamous slaughter of the innocents told in Matthew 2:16–18.

The English composer William Byrd (1543–1623) also memorialized this tragedy. Many consider Byrd the greatest English composer of any age, and some judge him the greatest composer of the Renaissance. Here is the first verse of his song to the little Jesus, "Lulla, My Sweet Little Baby":

Lulla, la lulla, lulla lullaby.
My sweet little baby, what meanest thou
    to cry?
Be still my blessed babe, though cause
    thou hast of mourn,
Whose blood most innocent to shed the
    cruel king hath sworn.
And lo, alas, behold what slaughter he
    doth make,
Shedding the blood of infants all, sweet
    Savior, for thy sake.
A King is Born, they say, which King
    this king would kill.
Oh woe, and woeful heavy day, when
    wretches have their will!

Although composed in the form of a lullaby, this is really a lament over the "woeful heavy day, when wretches have their will." When I look around the world today, a similar lament rises in my heart because wretches like King Herod still conduct royal intrigue and mass murder. But this season of the celebration of Jesus' birth also holds the hope of his Second Coming. For just as Herod's bloody rage could not prevent Christ's incarnation, nothing can hinder his return!

If you are like me and sometimes grieve that

THE CELEBRATION OF JESUS' BIRTH ALSO HOLDS THE HOPE OF HIS SECOND COMING.

latter-day Herods still slaughter the innocents, remember the Lord's promise, "Blessed are they that mourn: for they shall be comforted" (Matthew 5:4). And, amidst the feasts and lights of Christmas, offer this prayer for the Second Coming: "How long, O Lord, holy and true?" (Revelation 6:10).

NIGHT

Consider the setting of William Byrd's poem: An angel appears to Joseph and says, "Arise, and take the young child and his mother, and flee into Egypt, and be thou there until I bring thee word: for Herod will seek the young child to destroy him" (Matthew 2:13). Joseph arises in the dark of night, lights a lamp, rouses his wife, and whispers to her the angel's urgent, dreamlike message. They move quickly about the room, dressing, packing, planning. What do they take for the trip to Egypt? What must they abandon in Bethlehem?

Then the child awakens. Joseph kneels by

Jesus' little cot. "Lulla, la lulla, lulla lullaby," he sings in a whisper, his lips brushing the boy's warm forehead. Then Joseph tells God's Son what is to occur:

> Lulla, la lulla, lulla lullaby.
> My sweet little baby, what meanest
>   thou to cry?
> Lo, my little babe, be still, lament no more;
> From fury thou shalt step aside, help have
>   we still in store.
> We heavenly warning have some other
>   soil to seek,
> From death must fly the Lord of life, as
>   lamb both mild and meek.
> Thus must my babe obey the king that
>   would him kill.
> Oh woe, and woeful heavy day, when
>   wretches have their will.

Joseph's song to Jesus, as imagined by Byrd, remembers the extraordinary events of the boy's short life. He sings of the slaughter that is soon to come upon Bethlehem—a lullaby of murder and martyrdom. He weaves into the melody the strange story of the visitors from the East, whose gifts would soon be sold to finance the family's flight to safety. He recounts the shepherds' hurried visit—those rough men who were the first of the human race to hear of the Savior's birth.

MY SWEET LITTLE BABY, WHAT MEANEST THOU TO CRY?

"Lulla, la lulla, lulla lullaby. My sweet little baby, what meanest thou to cry?" The baby had plenty to cry about. While Joseph sang of the lovely mother who was to nurture "the Son of heavenly seed," armed soldiers were assembling nearby, preparing to kill him. But all the while, Joseph lilted the prophecies foretelling the baby's kingly life and reign and hustled the bundled mother and son out of Bethlehem toward Egypt—"Lulla, la lulla, lulla lullaby."

DECEMBER 8

Let this mind be in you, which was also in Christ Jesus: Who, being in the form of God, thought it not robbery to be equal with God: But made himself of no reputation, and took upon him the form of a servant, and was made in the likeness of men: And being found in fashion as a man, he humbled himself, and became obedient unto death, even the death of the cross. Wherefore God also hath highly exalted him, and given him a name which is above every name: That at the name of Jesus every knee should bow, of things in heaven, and things in earth, and things under the earth; and that every tongue should confess that Jesus Christ is Lord, to the glory of God the Father.

PHILIPPIANS 2:5–11

MORNING

This is as close as the apostle Paul comes to a Christmas story. But he cannot stop with the birth of Jesus; the apostle seems compelled to review the entire progress of Christ's life. Here is described the birth, life, death, resurrection, ascension, and Second Coming of the Lord. The essences of the four Gospels are compressed into 131 words of the King James Version. The traditional story of Christmas reveals prophecy of all this. Is it not worthwhile at this time of year to consider the outcome of the beautiful birth of Christ?

First, all apostles tell us who Jesus was: "Being in the form of God, [he] thought it not robbery to be equal with God" (Philippians 2:6). This is just as Matthew reported, "They shall call his name Emmanuel, which being interpreted is, God with us" (1:23). Or John, who said, "In the beginning was the Word. . .and the Word was God" (1:1). But Jesus did not cling to his equality with God when he appeared on the earth, and when people saw him, they had no idea that he was God.

The Savior didn't appear in a divine form. Rather the Son of God laid aside his glory and "made himself of no reputation, and took upon him the form of a servant, and was made in the likeness of men" (Philippians 2:7). These words describe exactly what happened when Jesus emerged from Mary's womb. As John said, "The Word was made flesh" (1:14).

CONSIDER THE OUTCOME OF THE BEAUTIFUL BIRTH OF CHRIST.

Then, for thirty years or so, Christ was "found in fashion as a man" (Philippians 2:8). In other words, he was no angel. He appeared to be like the common, sinful men around him. It is reported that when Joseph brought Mary and the boy back from Egypt, "he went and lived in a town called Nazareth. So was fulfilled what was said through the prophets: 'He will be called a Nazarene' " (Matthew 2:23 NIV). Not a god or a guru, simply a Nazarene.

A lovely hymn expresses the wonder of Christ becoming like us in order to save us. It was written by William Young Fullerton (1857–1932) and is sung to the tune "Londonderry Air" (the melody of "Danny Boy"). Here is the first verse of this hymn:

I cannot tell why he whom angels worship,
Should set his love upon the sons of men,
Or why, as Shepherd, he should seek
   the wanderers,
To bring them back, they know not how
   or when.
But this I know, that he was born of Mary
When Bethlehem's manger was his
   only home,

And that he lived at Nazareth and labored,
And so the Savior, Savior of the world
   is come.

NIGHT

God humbled himself to become a man—infinite condescension! But this is not all; "He humbled himself, and became obedient unto death, even the death of the cross" (Philippians 2:8). He not only took the form of man but the mortality of the flesh and died the most shameful and painful of all deaths, the death of crucifixion.

The magi's gift of myrrh, an embalming spice, pointed toward this death (Matthew 2:11). And the prophet Simeon told Mary of Jesus' death, saying, "Behold, this child is set for the fall and rising again of many in Israel; and for a sign which shall be spoken against" (Luke 2:34).

William Fullerton's hymn tells of Christ's death in more simple phrases:

> I cannot tell how silently he suffered,
> As with his peace he graced this place of tears,
> Or how his heart upon the cross was broken,
> The crown of pain to three and thirty years.
> But this I know, he heals the brokenhearted,
> And stays our sin, and calms our lurking fear,
> And lifts the burden from the heavy laden,
> For yet the Savior, Savior of the world is here.

Because Jesus died such a death, God lifted him up from the grave to the heavens, gave all power into his hands (Matthew 28:18), and made the humble name *Jesus* a name above every name (Philippians 2:10–11).

The incurious Jewish leaders of Jerusalem predicted this would happen, quoting to Herod the words of their own prophet: "And thou Bethlehem, in the land of Juda, art not the least among the princes of Juda: for out of thee shall come a Governor, that shall rule my people Israel" (Matthew 2:6).

No less an authority than Gabriel told Mary, "He shall be great, and shall be called the Son of the Highest: and the Lord God shall give unto him the throne of his father David: and he shall reign over the house of Jacob for ever; and of his kingdom there shall be no end" (Luke 1:32–33).

So Fullerton sings,

I cannot tell how he will win the nations,
How he will claim his earthly heritage,
How satisfy the needs and aspirations
Of East and West, of sinner and of sage.
But this I know, all flesh shall see his glory,
And he shall reap the harvest he has sown,
And some glad day his sun shall shine
    in splendor
When he the Savior, Savior of the world
    is known.

DECEMBER 9

And there were in the same country shepherds abiding

in the field, keeping watch over their flock by night.

And, lo, the angel of the Lord came upon them,

and the glory of the Lord shone round

about them: and they were sore afraid.

And the angel said unto them, Fear not:

for, behold, I bring you good tidings of great joy,

which shall be to all people.

For unto you is born this day in the city of David

a Saviour, which is Christ the Lord.

LUKE 2:8–11

 MORNING

I wonder if the shepherds were thinking about God that night of Christ's birth. It's possible that they were pious men who took advantage of the night watches to pray. Might they have been considering, hoping for, the birth of their Messiah?

These shepherds weren't the only ones of the Bible to receive a message from God. One day, long before, another shepherd was tending a flock on the back side of the Sinai desert. He doesn't seem to have been thinking of God at all. Still, the angel of the Lord appeared to Moses in a flame of fire from the midst of a bush. Moses' experience with that angel marked the beginning of Israel's salvation from Egypt (Exodus 3:1–12).

The shepherds near Bethlehem didn't see anything as simple as a burning bush. The glory of the Lord was *all around them,* and these hardworking men were afraid. As the angel was trying to calm them, "suddenly there was. . .a multitude of the heavenly host praising God, and saying, Glory to God in the highest, and on earth peace, good will toward men" (Luke 2:13–14). Imagine how this must have amazed them!

It is a credit to the courage and faith of these rough shepherds that they said to one another, "Let us now go even unto Bethlehem, and see this thing which is come to pass, which the Lord hath made known unto us" (Luke 2:15). So they went looking for this sign: a "babe wrapped in swaddling clothes, lying in a manger" (verse 12). How ordinary! This is like the dry desert bush that Moses saw. This is the way the Savior of the world was introduced.

After they had found Mary, Joseph, and Jesus, the shepherds told others what had happened and "all they that heard it wondered at those things" (Luke 2:18).

LET'S SEEK HIM IN

OUR ORDINARY LIVES,

God sometimes appears with angels or flames, but rarely. The next time this happens will be when Jesus comes again to be "revealed from heaven with his mighty angels" (2 Thessalonians 1:7). Meanwhile, let's seek him in our ordinary lives, lives like simple shepherds, where he is like a swaddled baby or a desert bush.

NIGHT

hrist has already been born, lived his life, and accomplished his purpose. So we can easily understand the words that predicted his birth. Isaiah makes perfect sense to us when he says, "Behold, a virgin shall conceive, and bear a son, and shall call his name Immanuel" (7:14). And, Micah 5:2 makes it obvious to us where the Messiah was to be born: "But thou, Bethlehem Ephratah, though thou be little among the thousands of Judah, yet out of thee shall he come forth unto me that is to be ruler in Israel; whose goings forth have been from of old, from everlasting."

But it wasn't so easy for people living two thousand years ago to understand these things. The Jewish leaders in Jerusalem didn't go with the wise men to seek the newborn king. Similarly, the people in Bethlehem who heard the news from the shepherds apparently didn't go to see him. In fact, most of the people in Israel missed out on the Lord's first appearing.

Believers in Christ can be thankful to God that they have seen the meaning of the birth of Christ. We did not miss it. Now we wait for another appearing of Jesus Christ—his Second Coming. What shall we do until he comes? We can care for the poor, preach the gospel, and work for justice. Plus, the Lord himself tells us in Luke 18 what he would like to find when he returns.

The first seventeen verses of Luke 18 tell two parables about prayer. When you read them, please notice the following half-verse tucked between the two parables: "Nevertheless when the Son of man cometh, shall he find faith on the earth?" (Luke 18:8). We each must answer this question for ourselves. "Will I be found faithful when the Lord returns?"

"WILL I BE FOUND

FAITHFUL WHEN

THE LORD RETURNS?"

I don't think these parables mean we all must literally be on our knees actively praying at the moment the Lord appears. What it does mean is that we can have an attitude that is inclined toward the Lord (1 Kings 8:58). A person with such faith can revert to prayer at any moment.

DECEMBER 10

And, behold, there was a man in Jerusalem, whose name was Simeon. . . . And he came by the Spirit into the temple: and when the parents brought in the child Jesus, to do for him after the custom of the law, then took he him up in his arms, and blessed God, and said, Lord, now lettest thou thy servant depart in peace, according to thy word: For mine eyes have seen thy salvation, which thou hast prepared before the face of all people; a light to lighten the Gentiles, and the glory of thy people Israel. And Joseph and his mother marvelled at those things which were spoken of him. And Simeon blessed them, and said unto Mary his mother, Behold, this child is set for the fall and rising again of many in Israel; and for a sign which shall be spoken against; (Yea, a sword shall pierce through thy own soul also,) that the thoughts of many hearts may be revealed.

LUKE 2:25, 27–35

MORNING

Each person who described Jesus near the time of his birth saw him as something different. Elizabeth, the mother of John the Baptist, called Jesus "my Lord" (Luke 1:43). Her husband Zechariah, in a rich prophetic vision, called Jesus a "horn of salvation" and the "dayspring from on high" (Luke 1:69, 78). And don't forget Mary, the young mother, who called her child God's gift of help to Israel (Luke 1:54).

The angel told the shepherds that the babe in the manger was the Savior of Israel (Luke 2:11). The wise men knew Jesus as the king of the Jews

(Matthew 2:2). Herod saw Jesus as a political rival and so tried to destroy him (Matthew 2:16–18). The old prophetess Anna saw in Jesus the redemption of Jerusalem (Luke 2:38).

This is the child of Christmas. He is the Lord, the dayspring from on high, and God's gift of help to Israel. Not only so, he is Israel's Savior and Messiah, the king of the Jews, the rival to a king, and the redemption of Jerusalem.

NOT ONLY GOD'S GIFT
TO ISRAEL, BUT A
BLESSING TO THE WHOLE WORLD.

Simeon, however, saw more in this divine baby boy than anyone else: He was not only God's gift to Israel, but a blessing to the whole world. Simeon understood what the others did not; that Christ was "prepared before the face of all people" (Luke 2:31). In other words, Jesus was not to be hidden in this distant province of the Roman Empire. He was not just the glory of Israel, but also "a light to lighten the Gentiles" (Luke 2:32). Simeon also knew the prophecies of Isaiah concerning the promised Messiah: "It is a light thing that thou shouldest be my servant to raise up the tribes of Jacob, and to restore the preserved of Israel: I will also give thee for a light to the Gentiles, that thou mayest be my salvation unto the end of the earth" (Isaiah 49:6).

And so, when Jesus came out of the wilderness to begin his ministry,

> He came and dwelt in Capernaum, which is upon the sea coast, in the borders of Zabulon and Nephthalim: That it might be fulfilled which was spoken by Esaias the prophet, saying, The land of Zabulon, and the land of Nephthalim, by the way of the sea, beyond Jordan, Galilee of the Gentiles; The people which sat in darkness saw great light; and to them which sat in the region and shadow of death light is sprung up.
>
> MATTHEW 4:13–16

NIGHT

Simeon told Mary and Joseph that the baby Jesus was the glory of God's people, Israel (Luke 2:32). It was an honor to the Jewish nation that the Messiah had come out of one of their tribes and would live and soon die among them. This glory will be theirs into eternity. "No longer will you need the sun or moon to give you light," declared Isaiah, "for the LORD your God will be your everlasting light, and he will be your glory" (Isaiah 60:19 NLT).

No wonder Joseph and Mary marveled at the things Simeon said about this boy! If that had been my baby, I would have been full of pride—"My child is the light of the Gentiles and the glory of Israel!"

But Simeon had more to say, which would temper whatever joy the child's parents may have felt, for he foretold of Jesus' death some thirty years later saying, "Behold, this child is set for the fall and rising again of many in Israel; and for a sign which shall be spoken against. . .that the thoughts of many hearts may be revealed" (Luke 2:34–35). With these words, Simeon again drew from Isaiah to describe the child.

Isaiah had said, "He shall be for a sanctuary; but for a stone of stumbling and for a rock of offence to both the houses of Israel, for a gin and for a snare to the inhabitants of Jerusalem. And many among them shall stumble, and fall, and be broken" (Isaiah 8:14–15). Does this sound like the Jesus people talk about at Christmas? It is none other than he. Jesus Christ was the stumbling stone for the Jews. The apostle Peter said that they stumbled because they disobeyed the gospel message (1 Peter 2:8). Gentiles, on the other hand, experienced Christ as a stepping-stone up out of darkness and into God's light (Ephesians 3:2–6).

D OES THIS SOUND
LIKE THE JESUS PEOPLE
TALK ABOUT AT CHRISTMAS?

Unlike the others, Simeon predicted the infant's death: "Yea, a sword shall pierce through thy own soul also" (Luke 2:35). This occurred some thirty years later as Mary stood by watching her beloved Jesus be crucified.

All this was said at Jesus' circumcision ceremony when the child was only eight days old.

DECEMBER 11

And there was one Anna, a prophetess,
the daughter of Phanuel,
of the tribe of Aser: she was of a great age,
and had lived with an husband
seven years from her virginity;
and she was a widow of about fourscore and four years,
which departed not from the temple,
but served God with fastings and prayers night and day.
And she coming in that instant
gave thanks likewise unto the Lord,
and spake of him to all them that
looked for redemption in Jerusalem.

LUKE 2:36–38

MORNING

Consider the scene at the temple in Jerusalem. The Word made flesh is held in young Mary's arms awaiting his circumcision. He who could claim equality with God has made himself nothing (Philippians 2:6–7). He and Mary are anonymous among a crowd of other newborns and mothers there for the same reason.

Joseph is there as well, holding two pigeons, the offering required by the Law of God for this ceremony. Yet he knows that the baby in his wife's embrace will be called Immanuel, which means *God with us* (Matthew 1:23). The temple designed for the worship of this same God surrounds the little family.

There the Christ-child is honored despite his anonymity. Two people acknowledge him. One is Simeon, who actually holds the baby in his arms. "Lord, now I can die in peace!" he prays. "I have seen the Savior" (Luke 2:29–30 NLT). Then he tells of the child's life and purpose: He will be the glory of Israel, the light of the Gentiles, and the cause of the falling and rising of many people. His mother's heart will break while her son is crucified as a sign from God that will be spoken against (see Luke 2:32–35).

A woman also bears testimony in this new beginning. She is the aged widow Anna, a prophetess constantly at prayer in the temple. Anna saw the baby, knew who he was, and did two things, which we should find helpful to remember.

First, Anna thanked God (Luke 2:38). A little thankfulness for the birth of Christ is a strong antidote to the excesses of the Christmas season. Try this in the mall, at the ATM machine, or when you've had too much fudge. Say a little prayer like Anna's: "Thank you, dear Father, that my eyes have seen your salvation!"

MY EYES HAVE SEEN
YOUR SALVATION!

Second, Anna spoke about the Christ-child to everyone who was looking for the redemption of Israel. This we can do as well. From time to time, as Christmas approaches, gently remind other believers, friends, and family: "There is born to you this day in the city of David a Savior, who is Christ the Lord" (Luke 2:11 NKJV).

NIGHT

Anna was always at the temple serving God with fasting and prayer, night and day. Have you noticed there are often women like Anna around, who are devout, with a mind to serve God, yet little known?

Long ago, when Moses was building the tabernacle, there were women who served at the door of that highly crafted tent (Exodus 38:8). Maybe we can understand Anna better by considering these women; it may also help us in finding Christ in Christmas.

Nothing much is said about the women in

Exodus, but we do know that they parted with their mirrors for use in fabricating the brass laver. Such mirrors were made of the finest brass, highly polished, and just the right material for the laver, which was a large bowl filled with water and set in a brass base. The priests used the laver to wash their hands and feet before they offered the sacrifices (Exodus 30:18–20).

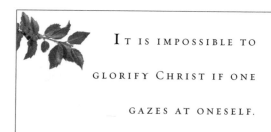

IT IS IMPOSSIBLE TO GLORIFY CHRIST IF ONE GAZES AT ONESELF.

We don't know how many ministering women gave their mirrors for the laver, but there must have been a good number of them because their mirrors were small, but the laver was big. These ancient women had somehow overcome their self-love. They no longer gazed at themselves in mirrors. They gave their mirrors up to make the worship of God possible, for without washing in the laver, the priests could not offer sacrifices (Exodus 30:21). In the same way, it is impossible to glorify Christ if one gazes at oneself in the mirror of this world. This is why, among all those who crowded the temple that day, Anna recognized Christ. She spent her life looking to God, not herself, and thus was blessed to be able to recognize the Savior immediately.

A Gospel story in Luke 7:36–50 illustrates this: A Pharisee once invited Jesus to supper. This man was blinded to the true identity of the Savior. He didn't offer water so Jesus could wash the dust from his feet. He didn't give him a kiss of greeting. He neglected the courtesy of olive oil to anoint his head. Though he had invited Jesus to a meal, he was ignoring him. Maybe this Pharisee was gazing at himself in a metaphorical brass mirror and thus looked completely past Jesus.

In contrast, a certain immoral woman heard Jesus was at the Pharisee's house and went there. She brought a beautiful jar filled with expensive perfume, knelt behind Jesus, and wept. Her tears fell on his feet, and she wiped them off with her hair. Then she continued, kissing his feet and putting perfume on them. This woman used her hair, her own glory (1 Corinthians 11:15), to wipe the dust off Jesus' feet. She could see Christ because she had no mirror, no self-glory.

DECEMBER 12

These things write I unto thee,

hoping to come unto thee shortly:

but if I tarry long,

that thou mayest know how thou oughtest

to behave thyself in the house of God,

which is the church of the living God,

the pillar and ground of the truth.

And without controversy great is the mystery of godliness:

God was manifest in the flesh,

justified in the Spirit, seen of angels,

preached unto the Gentiles,

believed on in the world, received up into glory.

1 TIMOTHY 3:14–16

MORNING

Last Christmas I saw a bumper sticker that said, "Keep the X in Xmas," mocking the saying "Keep Christ in Christmas." American Puritans, who tried to outlaw Christmas in the American colonies, would have liked the word *Xmas* because for them Christ was never in Christmas; to them it really was "Xmas."

During the past 120 years, Christmas has developed more and more into a holiday of overabundance and less and less as the season to remember the birth of our Savior. Previously it was more religious, a season carefully observed in liturgical worship by Episcopal and Lutheran churches. Christians did, and still do, celebrate the birth of Christ, but this is utterly snowed under by today's secular holiday. Can anyone get Christ back in Christmas?

When the apostle Paul wrote to his student and fellow apostle Timothy, he was concerned that people know how to live as Christians—how to live in the house of God, which is the church. The metaphor he used to describe the church may not explain how to keep Christ in Christmas, but it shows how we can keep Christ in the church—an even more important endeavor, I'd say.

Paul called the church "the pillar and ground of the truth" (1 Timothy 3:15). In other words, in this world, the church is the sole support of the truth. So let's ask Paul, "What is the truth?" He answers, "Great is the mystery of godliness" (1 Timothy 3:16).

The Christian faith is a mystery. This mystery can't be found out by reason because it is *above* reason. It is not a mystery of philosophy or speculation or science, but of *godliness*. It surpasses all other mysteries. Illogically, it is also a revealed mystery. It is no longer hidden or sealed. So elsewhere Paul wrote of his desire "to make all men see what is the fellowship of the mystery, which from the beginning of the world hath been hid in God" (Ephesians 3:9).

What is this revealed mystery? It is a person. It is Christ.

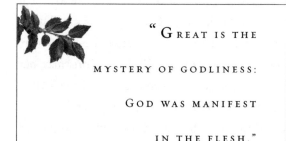

"GREAT IS THE MYSTERY OF GODLINESS: GOD WAS MANIFEST IN THE FLESH."

Today's verses from 1 Timothy are no less Christmas verses than the best of Luke and Matthew. In fact, they explain the accounts of the Gospels beginning with the birth of the baby Jesus, for "without controversy great is the mystery of godliness: God was manifest in the flesh" (1 Timothy 3:16).

NIGHT

To keep Christ in Christmas or any other season, the church must be the pillar and ground of the truth, lifting high the revealed mystery. Here is the mystery according to 1 Timothy 3:14–16: *God was manifest in the flesh.* When the time came for God to be revealed to humanity, he was born in a manger, the Word made flesh (John 1:14). But this is just the beginning!

God was *justified in the Spirit.* Although Christ was put to death in the body, the Spirit made him alive in resurrection. This justified his death and verified that God accepted Christ's death for our redemption (1 Peter 3:18).

Christ was *seen of angels.* They not only worshiped Christ (Hebrews 1:6), they were present at every step of his life—his incarnation, temptation, agony, death, resurrection, and ascension. The mystery of Christ is not only revealed to us on earth; angels see it as well.

Christ is *preached unto the Gentiles.* Before Christ, salvation was only for Jews (John 4:22). But God said to Christ, "It is too small a thing for you to be my servant to restore the tribes of Jacob and bring back those of Israel I have kept. I will also make you a light for the Gentiles, that you may bring my salvation to the ends of the earth" (Isaiah 49:6 NIV).

Christ was *believed on in the world.* The Gentiles welcomed the gospel that the Jews rejected. Amazing! Who could have imagined that the inhabitants of this world, which is under the control of the evil one (1 John 5:19 NIV), would believe in the Son of God and take him to be their Savior? Nonetheless, it is true.

Christ was *received up into glory* in his ascension. This happened before the world believed. It is put last because it was the finishing touch to his life. Now Jesus Christ is sitting at the right hand of God as our mediator, possessing all power in heaven and earth.

CHRISTIANS LOVE THIS GREAT MYSTERY AND BELIEVE IT.

Wonderful mystery of godliness! It is the full Christmas story—a mystery from beginning to end, from incarnation in the arms of Mary to ascension in the sight of the disciples. Christians love this great mystery and believe it.

Though we see this mysterious Christ through a glass, darkly, one day we will see him face-to-face, just like the apostle Paul, who said, "Now I know in part; but then shall I know even as also I am known" (1 Corinthians 13:12).

DECEMBER 13

But thou, Bethlehem Ephratah,

though thou be little among the thousands of Judah,

yet out of thee shall he come forth

unto me that is to be ruler in Israel;

whose goings forth have been from of old, from everlasting.

Therefore will he give them up,

until the time that she which travaileth hath brought forth:

then the remnant of his brethren shall

return unto the children of Israel.

And he shall stand and feed in the strength of the LORD,

in the majesty of the name of the LORD his God;

and they shall abide:

for now shall he be great unto the ends of the earth.

And this man shall be the peace.

MICAH 5:2–5

MORNING

When the wise men arrived in Jerusalem, they asked, "Where is he that is born King of the Jews? For we have seen his star in the east, and are come to worship him." The scribes paraphrased Micah 5:2 with great assurance: "And thou Bethlehem, land of Judah, art in no wise least among the princes of Judah: For out of thee shall come forth a governor, who shall be shepherd of my people Israel" (Matthew 2:6 ASV). It seemed to be well known among the Jews that Christ should come out of the town of Bethlehem where David lived (John 7:42).

Why do you think little Bethlehem should be the place of Christ's nativity? It is significant for at least two reasons. The first reason is bread. In the prophecy of Micah, Christ is standing and feeding the flock "in the strength of the LORD, in the majesty of the name of the LORD his God" (5:4). In Bethlehem, which means *the house of bread,* Jesus came down from heaven (John 6:51) to feed the human race with the bread of eternal life.

Christ still stands today, feeding us himself, the bread of heaven. "Whoever eats my flesh and drinks my blood has eternal life, and I will raise him up at the last day," says Jesus. "For my flesh is real food and my blood is real drink. . . . Just as the living Father sent me and I live because of the Father, so the one who feeds on me will live because of me. This is the bread that came down from heaven" (John 6:54–55, 57–58 NIV).

The second reason is the shepherd. The night of Christ's birth, shepherds heard this good news: "For unto you is born this day in the city of David a Saviour, which is Christ the Lord" (Luke 2:11). They hurried to Bethlehem when they heard this news. Bethlehem was called the city of David because it was formerly the home of David, who began as a shepherd and later became king of Israel (1 Samuel 16:11–13). The night of Jesus' birth, those shepherds greeted the birth of another shepherd (Matthew 2:6), "that great shepherd of the sheep" (Hebrews 13:20) who called himself "the good shepherd" (John 10:11). They found their Shepherd in Bethlehem as promised, but ironically lying in a manger, a feed trough for sheep and other livestock.

THEY FOUND THEIR SHEPHERD IN BETHLEHEM.

NIGHT

An angel told the shepherds exactly where to find the newborn Christ, in the city of David. Likewise the scribes in Jerusalem told the wise men that they would find the newborn king in Bethlehem. Jesus was born there in the former home of David, king of Israel, because he is the ruler of the kingdom of God, which is a continuation of David's kingdom. This is seen throughout Scripture and is an important part of the Christmas story. As Gabriel told Mary: "He shall be great, and shall be called the Son of the Highest: and the Lord God shall give unto him the throne of his father David: And he shall reign over the house of Jacob for ever; and of his kingdom there shall be no end" (Luke 1:32–33).

When Jesus was born, the royal line of David had been deposed from its throne for half a millennium. Yet God promised many times that David's kingdom would never end. For example, God promised Solomon, "I will establish the throne of thy kingdom upon Israel for ever, as I promised to David thy father" (1 Kings 9:5). Christ's birth fulfilled this promise.

Christians today live three thousand years after David. What does his kingdom have to do with us? It is the promised kingdom of the Messiah and we are the inheritors of the promises (Hebrews 6:12). What's more, Christ is the answer to all of God's promises (2 Corinthians 1:20). Not only so, the importance of David's kingdom in God's plan is expressed in the very first words of the New Testament, which are "The book of the generation of Jesus Christ, *the son of David*" (Matthew 1:1 emphasis added).

The wonder of Christmas is the birth of Christ, which marked the beginning of the establishment of God's kingdom on earth. The Old Testament calls this the kingdom of David. Because we believe in Jesus, who was born in the city of David, we've been called into this kingdom. And though the Jews do not yet see this as we do, the Scripture promises, "All Israel will be saved, as it is written: 'The deliverer will come from Zion; he will turn godlessness away from Jacob' " (Romans 11:26 NIV).

BECAUSE WE BELIEVE IN JESUS, WE'VE BEEN CALLED INTO THIS KINGDOM.

So, this Christmas season, we do well to remember the Lord's final words in Scripture: "I, Jesus. . .am the Root and the Offspring of David. . . . Yes, I am coming soon" (Revelation 22:16, 20 NIV).

DECEMBER 14

For unto us a child is born, unto us a son is given:

and the government shall be upon his shoulder:

and his name shall be called Wonderful,

Counsellor, The mighty God,

The everlasting Father, The Prince of Peace.

Of the increase of his government

and peace there shall be no end,

upon the throne of David, and upon his kingdom,

to order it, and to establish it with judgment and

with justice from henceforth even for ever.

The zeal of the LORD of hosts will perform this.

ISAIAH 9:6–7

MORNING

I saiah's inspiration draws together into one sentence the human and divine natures of our Savior. "For unto us a *child* is born, unto us a *son* is given" (Isaiah 9:6 emphasis added).

Jesus Christ was a child in his human nature, and so he was *born*. He was begotten of the Holy Spirit and delivered by Mary. The child was born—a child like any other woman or man that ever lived upon the face of the earth. The Nicene Creed explains this mystery like this: Christ "was made flesh of the Holy Spirit and the Virgin

Mary, and became man." Therefore Isaiah says that, in his humanity, the child was born.

But Jesus Christ is not only a man. He is God the Son. This is why Isaiah said that Christ the Son who was in the beginning with God (John 1:2) was *given* to us. This scriptural truth is very deep and difficult to express, yet it is the wonder of Christmas. Jesus Christ, as a man, was born. As God, he was *given*. What more can or should be said about this? This is the undoubted truth of our faith—the human and divine have come together in Christ. I cannot explain him further, for his mystery remains among the deep things of God. Although we humans cannot fathom this, we can rejoice in him.

THE HUMAN AND DIVINE HAVE COME TOGETHER IN CHRIST.

Faith is the evidence of the things that are not seen (Hebrews 11:1). We know Christ is truly human *and* divine. Beyond this, the mystery is outside our grasp because we are finite. Can an ant drink up the earth's oceans? If so, then a finite creature can comprehend the infinite God. But an understandable god would not be God, would not be infinite, would not be divine.

Still, at Christmas it is a joy to know Jesus Christ and to know that in all his mystery, he is the true godsend. "For God so loved the world, that he *gave* his only begotten Son, that whoso-ever believeth in him should not perish, but have everlasting life" (John 3:16 emphasis added).

NIGHT

Since we are like clueless ants drinking at the edge of an infinite ocean, what name shall we give to the child born, the Son given? Isaiah says, "His name shall be called Wonderful." And he *is* wonderful—our repository of astonishment and surprise, full of marvels and miracles, a child born, a son given—extraordinary, breathtaking!

Wonderful is a reasonable description for the man who is both human and divine. His wonderful love is displayed in his birth, life, death, resurrection, and ascension. Wonders constantly accompanied this man who is the mystery of godliness (1 Timothy 3:16).

Isaiah says that the child of Christmas is our Counselor. From eternity he was intimately acquainted with the counsels of God. Yet he promises, "I will instruct you and teach you in the way you should go; I will counsel you and watch over you" (Psalm 32:8 NIV). And those who seek this counsel testify, "You hold me by my right hand. You guide me with your counsel, and afterward you will take me into glory. Whom have I in heaven but you? And earth has nothing I desire besides you" (Psalm 73:23–25 NIV).

WONDERFUL, COUNSELOR, MIGHTY GOD, EVERLASTING FATHER, THE PRINCE OF PEACE.

What's more, he is called mighty God. Just as he embodies wisdom for counsel (1 Corinthians 1:30), so he is strength—our strength. "Therefore he is able to save completely those who come to God through him, because he always lives to intercede for them" (Hebrews 7:25 NIV).

The child born to us, the Son given to us, is called the everlasting Father. He is God, one with the Father who is from everlasting to everlasting (Psalm 90:2) and the author of eternal life (Acts 3:15)—the Father of eternity to all who believe.

Isaiah finally calls Christ the Prince of Peace. At Christmas, we often hear people wish for peace on earth. Pray this season that this world would no longer resist believing in the Prince of Peace who is himself our *only* peace (Ephesians 2:14). Therefore, "of the increase of his government and peace there will be no end. He will reign on David's throne and over his kingdom, establishing and upholding it with justice and righteousness from that time on and forever" (Isaiah 9:7 NIV).

DECEMBER 15

And the Word was made flesh, and dwelt among us,
(and we beheld his glory, the glory as of the
only begotten of the Father,) full of grace and truth.
John bare witness of him, and cried, saying,
This was he of whom I spake,
He that cometh after me is preferred before me:
for he was before me. And of his fulness
have all we received, and grace for grace.
For the law was given by Moses,
but grace and truth came by Jesus Christ.
No man hath seen God at any time;
the only begotten Son,
which is in the bosom of the Father,
he hath declared him.

JOHN 1:14–18

MORNING

J esus Christ's birth is called the *Incarnation*. It is the most important event in human history. There was never anyone like this man. Though he had mind and body and experienced joy and suffering like us (yet without sin), he was entirely God. This is such a mystery that even the inspired words of the Bible struggle to express it. Sometimes the Scriptures resort to literary devices like metaphor and analogy to help us understand the mystery of God, like the following story:

One day, an old man named Abraham and his

son, Isaac, trekked up a mountain called Moriah. Abraham carried a knife and hot coals for a fire. Isaac carried firewood. When they stopped to rest, Isaac said, "Father?"

"Yes, my son."

"We have the wood and the fire but where is the lamb for the sacrifice?"

Abraham answered, "My son, the Lord will provide a lamb" (see Genesis 22:5–8).

Three days before, God had told Abraham, "Take your son, your only son—yes, Isaac, whom you love so much—and go to the land of Moriah. Sacrifice him there as a burnt offering on one of the mountains, which I will point out to you" (Genesis 22:2 NLT). So Abraham, the father of faith, set off to do just this.

The end of this story reveals God in incarnation. Meanwhile let's look at how it reveals Abraham's faith, which carried the human race to the day of Christ's birth.

On a certain night before the birth of Isaac, God took Abraham outside and said, "Look up at the heavens and count the stars—if indeed you can count them. . . . So shall your offspring be"

(Genesis 15:5 NIV). That night Abraham "believed the LORD, and he credited it to him as righteousness" (Genesis 15:6 NIV). That night marked the beginning of faith in God's promises. But what if Abraham had killed Isaac? Then he wouldn't have even one son, much less numberless offspring like the stars in the sky. If Isaac were dead, God's promise, given on that starry night, would be nullified. But Abraham believed and continued to believe.

THE LORD WILL

PROVIDE A LAMB.

Picture Abraham and Isaac trudging up that slope. Isaac asks, "We have the wood and the fire, but where is the lamb for the sacrifice?"

The faithful old man answers, "My son, the Lord will provide a lamb." This story and this statement of faith describe the journey and hope of Israel, which reached its apex the day Gabriel told Mary, "And, behold, thou shalt conceive in thy womb, and bring forth a son, and shalt call his name JESUS. He shall be great, and shall be called the Son of the Highest: and the Lord God shall give unto him the throne of his father David: And he shall reign over the house of Jacob for ever; and of his kingdom there shall be no end" (Luke 1:31–33).

NIGHT

When Abraham and Isaac arrived at the mountaintop, Abraham built an altar and placed the wood on it. Then he bound Isaac and laid him on the altar over the wood. Abraham held the knife and lifted it to kill his son as a sacrifice to the Lord. In his heart he believed, *God will provide a lamb*. Suddenly the angel of the Lord called out of heaven, "Abraham, Abraham!"

The old believer calmly said, "Here I am."

"Lay down the knife," said the angel. "Do not hurt the boy, for now I know that you truly reverence God. You have not even held back your beloved son from me."

Abraham looked up from the altar where his son lay, and there, entangled by the horns in a thicket of brush, was a ram. This ram became the sacrifice in place of Isaac (see Genesis 22:9–13).

YOU HAVE NOT EVEN HELD BACK YOUR BELOVED SON FROM ME.

The ram was strong and powerful, but the instruments of his power, his horns, were caught in a thicket. This rendered him helpless, easily caught and sacrificed.

Isn't this ram like Christ? "Who, being in the form of God, thought it not robbery to be equal with God: but made himself of no reputation, and took upon him the form of a servant, and was made in the likeness of men: and being found in fashion as a man, he humbled himself, and became obedient unto death, even the death of the cross" (Philippians 2:6–8).

In the act of incarnation—of becoming the man Jesus—God became thoroughly entangled in the complex thicket of human existence. He was first a helpless baby, then a child. Finally, when Jesus was a man, people questioned, "If this is God in the flesh, why doesn't he display the power of God?" (see Matthew 16:1–4). Few people, if any, could see that in this man, God had provided a Lamb.

After his work on earth was complete, people brought the good news of Jesus into the world, and here is what they discovered:

> For the Jews require a sign, and the Greeks seek after wisdom: But we preach Christ crucified, unto the Jews a stumblingblock, and unto the Greeks foolishness; but unto them which are called, both Jews and Greeks, Christ the power of God, and the wisdom of God. Because the foolishness of God is wiser than men; and the weakness of God is stronger than men.
>
> 1 CORINTHIANS 1:22–25

December 16

God, who at sundry times and in divers manners spake in time past unto the fathers by the prophets, hath in these last days spoken unto us by his Son, whom he hath appointed heir of all things, by whom also he made the worlds; who being the brightness of his glory, and the express image of his person, and upholding all things by the word of his power, when he had by himself purged our sins, sat down on the right hand of the Majesty on high: being made so much better than the angels, as he hath by inheritance obtained a more excellent name than they. For unto which of the angels said he at any time, Thou art my Son, this day have I begotten thee? And again, I will be to him a Father, and he shall be to me a Son? And again, when he bringeth in the firstbegotten into the world, he saith, And let all the angels of God worship him.

Hebrews 1:1–6

MORNING

What are we celebrating at Christmastime? Everyone must know. Somewhere under blankets of entertainment and buying and selling and eating and drinking and dressing and decorating, we know of the precious child who rested in a manger.

Long ago Christians began to use this season as a time to remember, "When the fulness of the time was come, God sent forth his Son, made of a woman" (Galatians 4:4). But what does this really mean? The above verses from the book of Hebrews explain it: The way that God relates to humanity changed when that baby was born.

Before the nativity of Jesus, God spoke many times and in many ways through the prophets. What was the message? To Adam, it was that Christ would come from the seed of the woman (Genesis 3:15); to Abraham, that Christ would be his descendant (Genesis 22:18); to Jacob, that Christ would spring from the tribe of Judah (Genesis 49:8); to David, that Christ would be of his house (2 Samuel 7:16); to Micah, that Christ would be born at Bethlehem (Micah 5:2); to Isaiah, that Christ would be born of a virgin (Isaiah 7:14).

Hebrews 1:1 does not say that in the past God spoke at many times and in various ways about lots of things. No, God spoke about one thing—Christ. The Bible is about Christ and those who see this have found the key to understanding it.

GOD HAS SPOKEN

UNTO US BY AND

IN THE SON.

The days are past when the divine speaking was *about* Christ. In these last days God has spoken unto us *by* and *in* the Son. The babe in the manger is the speaking of God. He is also the message.

Hebrews calls these the last days because God's speaking in Christ is the final revelation. At first there was the revelation of God through the creation (Romans 1:20). Then came the dreams, visions, and voices seen and heard by the patriarchs (Genesis 12:1). Next came the Mosaic revelation in the Law (Exodus 20:1–18). At last, the prophets explained the Law and revealed more of the coming Christ (Isaiah 9:6–7).

Then the fullness of time came and God sent the Son, made of a woman (Galatians 4:4). He is the final revelation of God to us. In these days we enjoy the promised Spirit of truth who abides with us and lives in us to teach us all things and bring to our remembrance all that Christ did and said (John 14:16–17, 26).

NIGHT

At the birth of Jesus "a great company of the heavenly host appeared. . .praising God and saying, 'Glory to God in the highest, and on earth peace to men on whom his favor rests'" (Luke 2:13–14 NIV). I like the last words of this angelic praise—*peace to men on whom his favor rests*. God had not come to angels or any other creature but had favored humanity and even come *into* humanity in Christ.

The ancient prophets wanted to know about this. They foretold what God had prepared for us, even though they had questions about what it could mean. The Spirit of Christ within told them in advance about the Son's suffering and his glory afterward. They wondered at this and wanted to know when and to whom it would happen. They were told that these things would not happen during their lifetime, but years later. This is so wonderful that even the angels are watching, longing to look into these things (1 Peter 1:10–12).

"PEACE TO MEN ON WHOM HIS FAVOR RESTS."

Images of angels are favorites during Christmas. They appear as tree ornaments and house decorations. The real angels desire to know all about the person and work of the Son of God. But God's favor rests not on them; rather, God's favor rests on you and me. It is *our* privilege, among all creation, to know the Son of God!

Hebrews chapter one helps us better know the Son and how he stepped forward from eternity past to eternity future. First, before anything was made, God promised all to the Son as an inheritance. Then through the Son, God made the universe and everything in it (Hebrews 1:2). Throughout creation, the Son reflects God's glory and represents God exactly. As if this were not enough, the Son also sustains the universe by the power of his word. After he died to cleanse us from sin, he sat down in honor at the right hand of God's heavenly majesty (Hebrews 1:3).

This brings us up-to-date in the progress of God's beloved Son. The remainder of Hebrews 1 reveals more of Christ until a future day when he will roll up the creation like old clothes. It has perished, but he remains forever and his enemies have become a footstool under his feet (Hebrews 1:10–13).

DECEMBER 17

In the beginning was the Word,
and the Word was with God,
and the Word was God.

JOHN 1:1

Behold, a virgin shall be with child,
and shall bring forth a son,
and they shall call his name Emmanuel,
which being interpreted is, God with us.

MATTHEW 1:23

And, behold, thou shalt conceive in thy womb,
and bring forth a son, and shalt call his name JESUS.

LUKE 1:31

MORNING

Recently I was asked for my Social Security card, but I hadn't seen it for years. So I went to the Social Security office to get another one. Naturally, they needed proof that I am who I am. This was a problem because I had no valid identification showing my complete name. I've never used my complete name. With some effort, I eventually solved the problem, and now I have a little blue and white numbered card to prove it. You can be sure I'm much more careful about my name now!

Your name is a type of shorthand for who you

are and what you have done. For example, when you hear the name *Abraham Lincoln,* you think of the man who emerged from the American wilderness to become president and whose actions saved the Union. If you know the name *Emily Dickinson,* you think of a reclusive woman in a small New England town who wrote some of the best poetry in the English language.

In the beginning, the Word was with God (John 1:1), and John was somehow inspired to write about him. But John was slow to tell us the name of the one who is the Word. Suppose you were the first to read John's manuscript. Imagine your desire to find out who is the Word? You'd say, "He must have a name! I must find him!"

As you read John's Gospel, the apostle leads you from the beginning before all beginnings, tracking the Word—through whom all things were made, who is the life that is the light of men—all the way through rejection and acceptance. Yet he gives the Word no other name. You read on and see that the Word became flesh with the glory of the only begotten of the Father. Ah! He is now flesh. You're getting close! Without doubt he was given a name. "Who is this who is full of grace and truth," you ask; "whose fullness we have all received, even grace upon grace?" (see John 1:2–16).

YOU HAVE FOUND THE NAME ABOVE ALL NAMES.

Suddenly, in verse 17 you are told something you already know: "The law was given through Moses." Of course it was. Is nothing new? "But grace and truth [*grace and truth!*] came through Jesus Christ." Oh, finally! You have found the name above all names. It is Jesus Christ. He is the Word who was with God and is speaking from God to you, and to God for you (Hebrews 1:2; 1 Timothy 2:5).

NIGHT

An angel made sure that Mary and Joseph knew that the holy child to be born of Mary had a name. He told Joseph that the child would be known as Immanuel, meaning *God with us*. He told Mary to name the child Jesus, meaning *God is salvation* (Matthew 1:23; Luke 1:31).

Pity the people who use the name *Jesus Christ* as a curse—for them it has no meaning or power. When you hear someone use the Lord's name like this, pray for that person who has no idea of the indescribable marvel of it.

What does this name really mean? It means

that there is a man who, though he was God, did not cling to his rights as God. He made himself nothing; he took the position of a slave, appeared in human form, and humbled himself even further by dying a criminal's death on a cross (Philippians 2:6–8).

The name told Mary and the entire world that God became a man and lived a perfect life among us. His death reconciled the entire creation to God. And because he was resurrected from the dead, death was stripped of its power. Though many people have been presidents and many have been poets, not one has been or ever again will be what Jesus Christ is (see Colossians 1:14–20).

THE WORD *JESUS* HAS POWER THAT CANNOT BE EXAGGERATED.

Because of this, God raised Jesus up to the heights of heaven and gave him a name that is above every other name, so that at the name of

Jesus every knee will bow, in heaven and on earth and under the earth, and every tongue will confess that Jesus Christ is Lord, to the glory of God the Father (Philippians 2:9–11).

The word Jesus on the lips of a believer has power that cannot be exaggerated. Long ago some Christians were told, "Do you not know that the wicked will not inherit the kingdom of God? Do not be deceived: Neither the sexually immoral nor idolaters nor adulterers nor male prostitutes nor homosexual offenders nor thieves nor the greedy nor drunkards nor slanderers nor swindlers will inherit the kingdom of God" (1 Corinthians 6:9–10 NIV). Then they were bluntly informed, "That is what some of you were. *But* you were washed, you were sanctified, you were justified *in the name of the Lord Jesus Christ and by the Spirit of our God*" (1 Corinthians 6:11 NIV, emphasis added).

December 18

And the angel said unto them,
Fear not: for, behold, I bring you good tidings
of great joy, which shall be to all people.
For unto you is born this day in the city of David
a Saviour, which is Christ the Lord.
And this shall be a sign unto you;
Ye shall find the babe wrapped in swaddling clothes,
lying in a manger.
And suddenly there was with the angel
a multitude of the heavenly host praising God,
and saying, Glory to God in the highest,
and on earth peace, good will toward men.

Luke 2:10–14

MORNING

How many times have angels sung God's praises? I have no idea. They were present at the creation when "the morning stars sang together, and all the sons of God shouted for joy" (Job 38:7). At the end of time they'll be found chanting, "Blessing, and glory, and wisdom, and thanksgiving, and honour, and power, and might, be unto our God for ever and ever" (Revelation 7:12).

But when the angels saw that God had become a suckling infant upon a woman's breast, they reached for even higher notes. Singing "Glory to

God in the highest," the angel choir gave the most soaring praise for the most amazing divine accomplishment of all time.

I wonder if a call went out among the angels, summoning them to that field near Bethlehem, as recounted in the wonderful Christmas hymn of the Scotsman James Montgomery (1771–1854):

> Angels, from the realms of glory,
> Wing your downward flight to earth,
> Ye who sing creation's story,
> Now proclaim Messiah's birth.

I can just imagine how those multitudes of angels rushed to that place to sing "Glory to God in the highest" and add a wonderfully new phrase to the lexicon of faith: "Peace on earth, good will toward men." Since the day Adam and Eve were sent out from the garden, there had been no peace on earth, especially not in the human heart. But when that child was born, when that Son was given whose name is "the Prince of Peace" (Isaiah 9:6), those angels sang a new song, which is our gospel: "Peace on earth, good will toward men."

Some people picture God angrily throwing lightning bolts from his throne in heaven. Others see a cold, distant, uncaring God. But this is not who is revealed in the Bible. Can there be greater proof of God's loving-kindness toward us than the gift of his beloved Son, the Prince of Peace?

> CAN THERE BE
> GREATER PROOF OF
> GOD'S LOVING-KINDNESS?

Look around you at all the people bustling about on their Christmastime errands. Remember that God's good will has not come only to a select few, but to all humanity—even to those who curse God, who sin grievously against him, or who simply have not yet heard the gracious invitation: "Come now, and let us reason together. . .though your sins be as scarlet, they shall be as white as snow; though they be red like crimson, they shall be as wool" (Isaiah 1:18).

NIGHT

N ot only angels give glory to God. There is divine glory in every dewdrop that twinkles in the morning sun. That glory is magnified in every warbling bird. The entire creation is an instrument of God's praise. That's why the Scripture declares, "Let the heavens rejoice, and let the earth be glad; let the sea roar, and the fulness thereof. Let the field be joyful, and all that is therein: then shall all the trees of the wood rejoice before the LORD" (Psalm 96:11–13).

But creation, as unfathomable as it is, cannot sing a song as sweet and meaningful as that of God's

Incarnation! There is more melody in the baby Jesus lying in the manger than in all the galaxies that roll through God's unending universe. That child is the God-man. In him the Creator came into the creation; the eternal God was born as mortal man.

Creation plainly reveals God. "Since the creation of the world God's invisible qualities—his eternal power and divine nature—have been clearly seen, being understood from what has been made" (Romans 1:20 NIV). If people decide to ignore or deny God's existence, the testimony of creation gives them no excuse to do so. Yet the creation only expresses the Creator. In Christ, God is entirely and personally seen. He is "the radiance of God's glory and the exact representation of his being" (Hebrews 1:3 NIV).

The Son bears the true character of the Father,

IN CHRIST, GOD IS ENTIRELY AND PERSONALLY SEEN.

having the same image and likeness. In the power, wisdom, and goodness of Jesus Christ, we see the power, wisdom, and goodness of the Father—because the very nature and perfection of God are in him. That's why Jesus had the following conversation with his disciples, as recorded by John:

> "If you really knew me, you would
> know my Father as well. From now on,
> you do know him and have seen him."
> Philip said, "Lord, show us the Father
> and that will be enough for us." Jesus
> answered: "Don't you know me, Philip,
> even after I have been among you such
> a long time? Anyone who has seen me
> has seen the Father. How can you say,
> 'Show us the Father'?"
>
> JOHN 14:7–9 NIV

No wonder the multitude of the heavenly host praised God on the birthday of Jesus Christ! They understood the true wonder of Christmas: that in Jesus dwells all the fullness of the Godhead bodily (Colossians 2:9).

DECEMBER 19

For it is not possible that the blood of bulls
and of goats should take away sins.
Wherefore when he cometh into the world, he saith,
Sacrifice and offering thou wouldest not,
but a body hast thou prepared me:
in burnt offerings and sacrifices for sin
thou hast had no pleasure.
Then said I, Lo, I come
(in the volume of the book it is written of me,)
to do thy will, O God.

HEBREWS 10:4–7

MORNING

You might say, "I thought this was a book about Christmas. Why am I reading verses about the blood of bulls and goats, burnt offerings, and sacrifices for sin?" True, there is no tinsel and lights and artificial snow in these words. But I think one must get through such pretty things—open them like wrapping paper and ribbon to get at the gift of Christmas. Real joy can be found in Christmas when one drops the last syllable of the word—*mas*—and finds Christ.

These verses show the glory of Christmas

without the -*mas*: "Sacrifice and offering you did not desire, but a body you prepared for me. . . . I said, 'Here I am—it is written about me in the scroll—I have come to do your will, O God'" (Hebrews 10:5–7 NIV).

The days depicted in the Old Testament were full of animal sacrifices. These were ordained in the Law of Moses because the blood of bulls and goats took away sin. The truth is, as mentioned earlier in Hebrews 10, these sacrifices were only a shadow of things to come (verse 1). The person casting that shadow was Christ. He is the real sacrifice for sin. The shadow-sacrifices, the bulls and goats, were only meant to indicate that Christ would indeed come.

CHRIST IS THE REAL SACRIFICE FOR SIN.

Those shadowy sacrifices were repeated again and again, year after year, but they never provided perfect cleansing for those who came to worship.

If they had, the sacrifices would have stopped; the worshipers would have been purified from sin forever. This is explained in Hebrews 10:1–4.

Now, under the gospel, good things have come. The redemption is perfect, never to be repeated. You and I, the pardoned sinners, never need be pardoned again. A simple renewal of repentance and faith invariably provides the comfortable sense of God's continued pardon. This is the gift of Christmas!

NIGHT

Isaac Watts (1674–1748), the great English hymn writer, composed these words:

Not all the blood of beasts
On Jewish altars slain
Could give the guilty conscience peace
Or wash away the stain.

But Christ, the heav'nly Lamb,
Takes all our sins away;
A sacrifice of nobler name
And richer blood than they.

What makes Christ's blood nobler and richer than the sacrifices that God ordained in the Law? I'll explain it like this: A debt has to be paid back in kind. That means that when you borrow a cup of sugar, you pay it back with sugar; borrow a U.S. dollar, pay back a U.S. dollar. Human sin requires human blood for redemption. Those animal sacrifices didn't take away sin because they didn't have the same nature as the sinner. But Jesus Christ was human, so His redeeming blood is nobler and richer.

Why not require the blood of the one who sinned? That blood is human. True, but it is the blood of a sinner that can't take away sin. The perfect God requires a perfect sacrifice. "Bring to the LORD a young bull without defect as a sin offering," says the Law (Leviticus 4:3 NIV). The only man who is sinless, without defect, is Jesus Christ. So the one who had no sin was made a sin offering for us (2 Corinthians 5:21).

All this talk about blood and sin at Christmastime can't be avoided. The Son himself said, "A body you prepared for me" (Hebrews 10:5 NIV). That is the body of the baby in the manger, which grew to be the body of the man on the cross. And that man said, "I have come to do your will, O God" (Hebrews 10:7 NIV). He was perfectly suited to satisfy divine justice.

THE ONE WHO HAD NO SIN WAS MADE A SIN OFFERING FOR US.

In the ancient days, the one bringing the sin offering would lay his hand on the head of the sacrifice as it was slain (Leviticus 4:4). Today, what the blood of that creature could not do, the blood of Christ has done and still does. It takes away sin from the sight of God and from the conscience of the believer. This is why we sing with Isaac Watts,

My faith would lay her hand
On that dear head of thine,
While, like a penitent, I stand,
And there confess my sin.

Believing, I rejoice
To see the curse remove;
I bless the Lamb with cheerful voice,
And sing his bleeding love.

DECEMBER 20

That which was from the beginning, which we have heard,
which we have seen with our eyes,
which we have looked at and our hands have touched—
this we proclaim concerning the Word of life.
The life appeared; we have seen it and testify to it,
and we proclaim to you the eternal life,
which was with the Father and has appeared to us.
We proclaim to you what we have seen and heard,
so that you also may have fellowship with us.
And our fellowship is with the Father
and with his Son, Jesus Christ.

1 JOHN 1:1–3 NIV

MORNING

At Christmas we celebrate the beginning of the gospel when the Word became flesh (John 1:14), when "that holy thing" was begotten in Mary (Luke 1:35), and the Savior was born in the city of David (Luke 2:11). This is the moment when the Word of life appeared. Yet this beginning, which itself is beyond description, draws us to contemplate another beginning, which is before all beginnings, when Jesus Christ, in his divine nature, existed as the everlasting God. Astonishing! John saw with his own eyes and touched with his own hands "that which was from the beginning."

AT CHRISTMAS WE CELEBRATE THE BEGINNING OF THE GOSPEL.

In that beginning, long before John and the apostles, before the prophets, before Abraham and Adam, and before all creatures, there was someone. Someone existed before the creation of the world. In him all things were created (Colossians 1:16), and he is from everlasting (Micah 5:2). This is the one whom the Father loved before the foundation of the world (John 17:24) when God's elect were chosen in him (Ephesians 1:5). He is the perfect Lamb who was chosen before the creation of the world and was revealed for your sake (1 Peter 1:20). This is the man seen and heard and proclaimed by John, this Word of life, who told him, "Blessed are your eyes because they see, and your ears because they hear. For I tell you the truth, many prophets and righteous men longed to see what you see but did not see it, and to hear what you hear but did not hear it" (Matthew 13:16–17 NIV).

Yes, John heard a voice from heaven and saw Christ gloriously transfigured (Matthew 17:2, 5). But even better, he heard Christ's voice in private conversation and in public discourse. He saw his common actions like eating, drinking, walking, and sleeping. He also was there to see him raise the dead, cleanse the lepers, restore sight to the blind, cause the lame to walk, the dumb to speak, and the deaf to hear. And John saw Jesus hanged upon the cross. He saw the one who is from everlasting bleeding and dying. He heard him sigh, "It is finished." John entered the empty tomb after Christ's resurrection from the dead and was with him for forty days afterward. John was among those who stood and gazed as Jesus Christ, who is from the beginning, was taken up and returned to the Father (Acts 1:9).

NIGHT

The apostles knew the one who was from the beginning. They knew him very well and were able to describe his stature, features, and the lineaments of his body. Their hands had even felt this Word of life!

Peter grasped Christ's hand when he lost faith while walking on water (Matthew 14:29–31). John leaned his head on Jesus' bosom (John 13:23). Thomas, after the resurrection, put his fingers into the Lord's wounds (John 20:27). Similarly, Jesus invited all the apostles to touch him when he appeared to them after his resurrection (Luke

24:39), proving that it was he and not a phantom without flesh and bones.

This Word of life was manifest in the flesh, born in Bethlehem as the Savior, Christ the Lord. We celebrate his birth knowing it was the birth of the author of life (Acts 3:15 NIV). But we also celebrate because Jesus does not just belong to those who knew him during his life on this earth. John proclaimed what he had seen and heard so that we can have fellowship with him. Thus, he invites us into fellowship with the Father and with his Son, Jesus Christ (1 John 1:3).

The gospel of Jesus Christ is shown during the Christmas season in his marvelous birth. Our faith is our ticket into a universal fellowship with God in the Son. In fact, whoever has responded in faith to the gospel message has been called into this fellowship (1 Corinthians 1:9), which includes every believer there ever was and ever will be. Fellowship is like a river in which we freely enjoy the refreshing love of God, the grace of Christ, and the fellowship of the Holy Spirit (2 Corinthians 13:14 NIV).

Jesus promised to us the water that takes away

thirst altogether and becomes a perpetual spring within us, giving eternal life (John 4:14). One day he even stood up in the temple and shouted about it: "If anyone thirsts, let him come to Me and drink. He who believes in Me, as the Scripture has said, out of his heart will flow rivers of living water" (John 7:37–38 NKJV).

OUR FAITH IS OUR TICKET INTO FELLOW-SHIP WITH GOD IN THE SON.

This invitation into the river of God's fellowship continues to the end when, "The Spirit and the bride say, 'Come!'. . . . Whoever wishes, let him take the free gift of the water of life" (Revelation 22:17 NIV).

DECEMBER 21

The first man is of the earth, earthy;
the second man is the Lord from heaven.
As is the earthy, such are they also that are earthy:
and as is the heavenly,
such are they also that are heavenly.
And as we have borne the image of the earthy,
we shall also bear the image of the heavenly.

1 CORINTHIANS 15:47–49

 MORNING

Think of the biblical images that appear most in popular culture. There are four by my count: Adam and Eve, Noah and the ark, the birth of Jesus, and his death. Adam was the beginning, and Noah passed through the judgment of the flood. The birth of Jesus was the new beginning, and in his death he passed through the judgment of the cross. These beginnings cannot be separated from their ends. Likewise, we who know Christ in his birth know him in his death.

Scripture also makes an unbreakable link

between the two beginnings—that of Adam and that of Christ. Since this is the season to remember the birth of Christ, let's look at the other beginning.

The first man was formed of dust, which in Hebrew signifies *red earth* (Genesis 2:7). Named Adam, meaning *red,* he cared for the Garden and was given dominion over the earth and sea (Genesis 1:26). Then sin entered and Adam was thrust from the Garden to toil in the same earth from which he was taken and for which he was named. "By the sweat of your brow you will eat your food until you return to the ground," said his Creator, "for dust you are and to dust you will return" (Genesis 3:19 NIV).

Everyone born since then is doomed to return to dust. Adam's sin and fall has pervaded the bodies and souls of all his descendants, making us sensual and earthy—that is, we naturally mind and cleave to earthly things. I think this explains the popularity of the Christmas season among those who don't believe in Christ. With parties and gifts and good food and many other types of overindulgence, it is the topmost time to be like the first man—that is, "of the earth, earthy."

But the second man is the Lord from heaven. Adam was the first man; Christ is the second. Today's reading from 1 Corinthians speaks of them as if they were the only two men in the world. The first was the head and representative of all his natural offspring. Likewise, the second is the head and representative of all his spiritual offspring.

CHRIST, THE SON OF GOD, CAME FROM HEAVEN IN INCARNATION.

Formed under the overshadowing of the Holy Spirit out of the substance of Mary, Jesus' body was indeed earthy. It was supported by earthly means and at its end was interred in the earth. In this way Christ, the Son of God, came from heaven in incarnation and entered into union with the human nature. This describes the believer's reason for celebrating Christmas.

NIGHT

We observe Christmas because the church has marked this as the time when the second man, the Son of God, came from heaven and entered into union with the human nature. Yet there are still two men in this world, one of the earth and the other of heaven—Adam and Christ. Every man and woman is included in one or the other.

Everyone has an earthly body. Just like Adam's, your body is a house of clay. The apostle Paul called his the "earthly house of this tabernacle" (2 Corinthians 5:1). It rises out of the earth, is maintained by the things of it, and returns to it again. In other words, "As is the earthy, such are they also that are earthy"; but that's not all, and this is the wonder of Christmas: "As is the heavenly, such are they also that are heavenly" (1 Corinthians 15:48). Just as you are now like Adam, the man of the earth, so you will someday be like Christ, the man from heaven. So, speaking to believers in Christ, Scripture says, "Set your minds on things above, not on earthly things. For you died, and your life is now hidden with Christ in God. When Christ, who is your life, appears, then you also will appear with him in glory" (Colossians 3:2–4 NIV).

Christ, the second man, now has a glorious and spiritual body. As certainly as he was born of Mary, he will descend from heaven in his Second Coming. Your faith in the Lord from heaven makes you a partaker of the heavenly calling (Hebrews 3:1). You are a citizen of heaven (Philippians 3:20 NIV). This means that on that resurrection morning, you will have a heavenly, spiritual, and glorious body like Christ's!

The following is God's promise given in the birth of Jesus Christ, the second man, the Lord from heaven: "As we have borne the image of the earthy, we shall also bear the image of the heavenly" (1 Corinthians 15:49).

"WE SHALL ALSO BEAR THE IMAGE OF THE HEAVENLY."

For now we must live in the image of the earthy. But this does not prevent our being rooted and established in love as we grasp the width and length and height and depth of Christ's love. We only bear the image of the first man until we fully know the love that surpasses knowledge and are utterly filled with God. Then our bodies are fashioned in the heavenly image and likeness of Christ (see Ephesians 3:14–21).

DECEMBER 22

The book of the generation of Jesus Christ,
the son of David,
the son of Abraham.

MATTHEW 1:1

I Jesus have sent mine angel to testify unto you
these things in the churches.
I am the root and the offspring of David,
and the bright and morning star.

REVELATION 22:16

Now to Abraham and his seed were the promises made.
He saith not, And to seeds, as of many;
but as of one, And to thy seed, which is Christ.

GALATIANS 3:16

 M O R N I N G

Genesis begins with four chapters that comprise the book of the generation of the world—creation and the birth of human culture. Chapter five of Genesis is called *The book of the generations of Adam* (v. 1).

The New Testament is a new book that tells of the last Adam (1 Corinthians 15:45). So the Gospel of Matthew is titled *The book of the generation of Jesus Christ* (1:1). It is the story of the one who created the world, breathed the breath of life into Adam, was born into the creation, and redeemed it from Adam's fall.

The story begins with a familiar name—*the son of David.* Well-educated scribes and Pharisees of that day knew the Messiah by this name, as did the common people (Matthew 12:23; 22:42). But the house of David was buried in obscurity by the time Jesus was born. How could they imagine the Messiah coming out of David's family? Yet, "The LORD hath sworn in truth unto David; he will not turn from it; Of the fruit of thy body will I set upon thy throne. . . . For the LORD hath chosen Zion; he hath desired it for his habitation" (Psalm 132:11, 13).

H IS THRONE IS FOR ALL GENERATIONS.

David, the king who was "ruddy, with a fine appearance and handsome features" (1 Samuel 16:12 NIV) had been dead for half a millennium. And so the Messiah truly came "as a root out of a dry ground" (Isaiah 53:2).

God said, "I have sworn unto David my servant, Thy seed will I establish for ever, and build up thy throne to all generations" (Psalm 89:3–4). This is a big promise that goes far beyond the little nation of Israel. It concerns the child who would be born and the Son given—the one we adore in the Christmas season. The government of David would rest upon his shoulders (Isaiah 9:6). But his throne is for *all* generations, so he is the mighty God, the everlasting Father, and the Prince of Peace.

NIGHT

J esus Christ is not only the son of David, but also the son of Abraham (Genesis 17:5). This shows that God is faithful to his promise and will make good every word that he has spoken. So, we who read the first sentence of the New Testament can be assured of its fulfillment to the end.

God promised Abraham a son who would be the great blessing of the world (Genesis 22:17) The patriarch might have expected this would be his immediate son. But it proved to be the child we revere at Christmastime—born forty-two generations after the promise was given. God fulfilled what was promised long after it was foretold. This excruciating delay in accomplishment of the divine plan exhausted human patience but did not weaken God's promise.

G OD IS FAITHFUL

TO HIS PROMISE.

The first few words of the New Testament describe the meaning of all history. They reiterate God's pledge to David of an eternal kingdom and the guarantee to Abraham of an everlasting family. Though I rarely hear these things mentioned in all the talk at Christmastime, they are the reason the angels could not be restrained on the day of Christ's birth: "And suddenly there was with the angel a multitude of the heavenly host praising God, and saying, Glory to God in the highest, and on earth peace, good will toward men" (Luke 2:13–14).

God's time for the carrying out of his promises came when it was most improbable. The glory of David's kingdom was dull as dust, and Abraham's expectation of a blessed son was two thousand years old. Today we are equally distant from the days of Christ as were first-century Jews from the days of Abraham. Scripture foresaw this, giving this advice:

> In the last days there will be scoffers who will laugh at the truth and do every evil thing they desire. This will be their argument: "Jesus promised to come back, did he? Then where is he? Why, as far back as anyone can re-member, everything has remained exactly the same since the world was first created." . . .But you must not forget, dear friends, that a day is like a thousand years to the Lord, and a thousand years is like a day. The Lord isn't really being slow about his prom-ise to return, as some people think. No, he is being patient for your sake. He does not want anyone to perish, so he is giving more time for everyone to repent.
>
> 2 PETER 3:3–4, 8–9 NLT

DECEMBER 23

And it came to pass in those days,

that there went out a decree from Caesar Augustus,

that all the world should be taxed.

(And this taxing was first made when

Cyrenius was governor of Syria.)

And all went to be taxed, every one into his own city.

And Joseph also went up from Galilee,

out of the city of Nazareth, into Judaea,

unto the city of David, which is called Bethlehem;

(because he was of the house and lineage of David:)

to be taxed with Mary his espoused wife,

being great with child. And so it was, that,

while they were there, the days were accomplished

that she should be delivered.

LUKE 2:1–6

MORNING

Scripture often mentions that God preset a time for Christ to live among us. There was a time for his birth: "When the fulness of the time was come, God sent forth his Son, made of a woman" (Galatians 4:4); a time for him to preach: Jesus said, "The time is fulfilled, and the kingdom of God is at hand: repent ye, and believe the gospel" (Mark 1:15); a time for his death: "Who gave himself a ransom for all, to be testified in due time" (1 Timothy 2:6); and the right time for the spreading of the gospel: "But hath in due times manifested his word through preaching" (Titus 1:3).

King David prophesied of this, saying, "You will arise and have compassion on Zion, for it is time to show favor to her; the appointed time has come" (Psalm 102:13 NIV). The apostle Paul called this period "the dispensation of the fulness of times" (Ephesians 1:10). As we observe Christmas, we actually celebrate the coming of the fullness of times.

> **WE CELEBRATE THE COMING OF THE FULLNESS OF TIMES.**

What if Christ had come immediately after Adam's fall? The enormity of the separation from God would not have been fully realized. We would not have altogether tasted the deadly fruit of sin or felt in desperation our need for the Savior. In the fullness of times, sin and death were fully developed.

Man's inability to find salvation by obedience

to the law was also manifested. Whether the law of God or the rule of conscience, it didn't matter—we'd failed. So the moral world was divinely prepared. Plus, the prophecies of various ages centered on this particular time.

Finally, Luke tells that the social and political stage was set for the entrance of the Redeemer. Caesar Augustus (63 B.C.–A.D. 14) was the second emperor of Rome, inheriting the position in 27 B.C. from his uncle Julius Caesar (100–44 B.C.). His original name, Thurinus, was changed to Augustus, meaning *exalted*, after he became Caesar.

Augustus presided over a remarkable twenty years of peace within the empire. This came after an era of vicious civil wars, and so the grateful Romans awarded him the title Pater Patriae, *father of his country*, in 2 B.C. The peace allowed Augustus to decree a census of the empire in order to secure his ability to impose taxes. By the providence of God, the man Joseph and his pregnant wife made their way to Bethlehem in obedience to the decree. There the true exalted one was born.

NIGHT

About 30 B.C., when Caesar Augustus was living in Spain, he intended to take a count of the inhabitants of the empire. But he was distracted from this by disturbances in the realm and his competition with the Roman senate for power. Also, unbeknownst to anyone, this was not the fullness of time. Had the census been taken then, it probably would not have been done later and the inn at Bethlehem would not have received Mary and Joseph. But things were ordered by an all-wise Providence, "And Joseph also went up from Galilee. . .unto the city of David, which is called Bethlehem. . .to be taxed with Mary his espoused wife" (Luke 2:4–5).

The decree was for the entire world to be taxed. A lot of trouble was taken to accomplish this, though not for the purpose of an earthly kingdom. It was all done to bring a pregnant young woman to the right place at the right time.

Early Christians did not record the date of Christ's birth. The earliest mention of December 25 came in the fourth century. The Eastern Church, centered in Constantinople (now Istanbul, Turkey), at first celebrated Christ's birth in a feast called Epiphany, which means *manifestation*. They chose January 6 as the date for this feast, reasoning that since the first Adam was born on the sixth day of creation, the birth of the last Adam (1 Corinthians 15:45) should be celebrated on the sixth day of the year. The Western Church was centered in Rome. It celebrated Christ's birth on the twenty-fifth of December. The Christian origins of this feast, called Natalis, meaning *nativity,* are lost to history. Eventually Pope Julius I (337–352) designated December 25 as the proper day for the entire church. With the coming of the Reformation, Protestant churches continued the tradition.

"GOD SENT FORTH HIS SON, MADE OF A WOMAN."

Some Christians complain about the impure origin of the Christmas celebration. A pope chose its date; its decorated trees and wreaths and a supernatural character named Santa Claus all have pagan beginnings. But none of this really matters—our faith is what matters. It makes us sure of what we hope for and certain of what we do not see (Hebrews 11:1). So, by faith let's sanctify our hearts with this truth: "When the fulness of the time was come, God sent forth his Son, made of a woman" (Galatians 4:4).

DECEMBER 24

But when Herod was dead, behold, an angel of the Lord
appeareth in a dream to Joseph in Egypt, saying,
Arise, and take the young child and his mother,
and go into the land of Israel: for they are dead
which sought the young child's life. And he arose,
and took the young child and his mother, and came
into the land of Israel. But when he heard that
Archelaus did reign in Judaea in the room of his father
Herod, he was afraid to go thither: notwithstanding,
being warned of God in a dream, he turned aside into
the parts of Galilee: and he came and dwelt in a city
called Nazareth: that it might be fulfilled which was
spoken by the prophets, He shall be called a Nazarene.

MATTHEW 2:19–23

MORNING

Christ put aside the Godhead and came to live in the confusing human world. Immediately upon his birth, this confusion whirled around him. Joseph was a good man but could not understand what was happening, so God instructed him through dreams. When danger in Bethlehem threatened the baby Jesus, Joseph took him to live in Egypt. Acting on another dream, the family returned to Judea. Then, a third dream diverted them to Nazareth. Prophecy said that the Messiah would be born in Bethlehem (Micah 5:2), but everyone knew him as a Nazarene. How puzzling!

No wonder the disciples gave the wrong answer when Jesus asked, "Who do people say that I am?"

"Some say John the Baptist," they replied, "some say Elijah, and others say Jeremiah or one of the other prophets" (see Matthew 16:13–14).

People also insultingly called Jesus a drunkard, a friend of sinners, and a criminal. They obviously didn't know who he was. Even the citizens of Jesus' hometown said, "He's just a carpenter's son, and we know Mary, his mother, and his brothers—James, Joseph, Simon, and Judas. All his sisters live right here among us. What makes him so great?" (Matthew 13:55–56 NLT).

The same is true to this day. People simply don't know who Jesus is. What is the remedy for this? When Jesus asked the disciples, "Who do you say I am?" Simon Peter answered, "You are the Messiah, the Son of the living God." Jesus replied, "You are blessed. . .because my Father in heaven has revealed this to you. You did not learn this from any human being" (see Matthew 16:15–17 NLT).

The story of the baby in the manger did not spring from the human imagination. This event is beyond the grasp of the most exalted and refined reasoning. It is something that eye has not seen, nor ear heard, nor has it entered into the mind of man to conceive. The light of nature and force of reason are helpless to understand it.

THIS EVENT IS BEYOND THE GRASP OF THE MOST EXALTED REASONING.

The gospel is a heavenly revelation. Yes, one can understand by the testimony of creation that there is a God—there a seeker can see the living God who gives life and breath and all things to his creatures. But to see that the Son has been given, who is of the same nature with God and equal to God, who is the Messiah of Israel and the Savior of lost sinners, is impossible unless the Father reveals it.

NIGHT

I was raised in a family that always went to church. I attended Sunday school and later was active in the youth group, but in all that time, I never saw the true identity of the baby in that manger. One night, when I was twenty-four years old, "It pleased God, who separated me from my mother's womb, and called me by his grace, to reveal his Son in me" (Galatians 1:15–16). Christmas has never been the same for me since then.

The revelation of Christ is the heart of Scripture. The Bible says this is "the mystery which hath been hid from ages and from generations, but now is made manifest to his saints. . .which is Christ in you, the hope of glory" (Colossians 1:26–27). This revelation of Christ decodes the Bible. It all makes sense when you see Christ. Even the apostle Paul had to admit, "Once I mistakenly thought of Christ that way, as though he were merely a human being. How differently I think about him now!" (2 Corinthians 5:16 NLT).

"CHRIST IN YOU, THE HOPE OF GLORY."

But this is not a one-time event, this revelation of Jesus Christ. As one continues to read and pray in the Scriptures, the vision becomes more wonderful. Even the apostle John, who saw the story unfold from beginning to end, had not seen all of Christ. When he was an old man, he testified, "I was in the Spirit on the Lord's day, and heard behind me a great voice, as of a trumpet, saying, I am Alpha and Omega, the first and the last: and, What thou seest, write in a book" (Revelation

1:10–11). The book he wrote is the final one in the Bible. It is called *The Revelation of Jesus Christ.*

Paul prayed for you to have this revelation: "[I] cease not to give thanks for you, making mention of you in my prayers; that the God of our Lord Jesus Christ, the Father of glory, may give unto you the spirit of wisdom and revelation in the knowledge of him" (Ephesians 1:16–17). If you wish, you can continue Paul's prayer so that Christ will be revealed to yourself and to others: "Oh, God of my Lord Jesus Christ, Father of glory, give me a spirit of wisdom and revelation in the full knowledge of your Son. Enlighten the eyes of my understanding so that I can know what is the hope of his calling and what are the riches of the glory of his inheritance in the saints" (see Ephesians 1:18–19).

DECEMBER 25

Hast thou eaten of the tree, whereof I commanded
thee that thou shouldest not eat? And the man said,
The woman whom thou gavest to be with me, she gave
me of the tree, and I did eat. And the LORD God
said unto the woman, What is this that thou hast done?
And the woman said, The serpent beguiled me, and
I did eat. And the LORD God said unto the serpent,
Because thou hast done this, thou art cursed above all
cattle, and above every beast of the field; upon thy
belly shalt thou go, and dust shalt thou eat all the days
of thy life: and I will put enmity between thee
and the woman, and between thy seed and her seed;
it shall bruise thy head, and thou shalt bruise his heel.

GENESIS 3:11–15

MORNING

Every family has its stories. My aunt recently told my daughter about the tornado in Washington, Kansas. It came through the center of town during a celebration on July 4, 1932, destroying the county courthouse. My aunt took refuge in the fruit cellar of her grandmother's house. When she emerged, the house no longer had a roof, and the winds had dropped the water tank from the railroad yard on my great-grandfather's storage shed.

I treasure my family's stories, though they may have little meaning to anyone else; like the one about my father's dog, Shy Violet, who protected him from rattlesnakes when he was a boy in Oklahoma. The dog was bitten so often that it was immune to the snakes' venom.

The family of man shares many stories. The most tragic one tells of our fall away from God. It resonates with meaning for all humanity. This meaning is expressed in the Christmas story.

As I reread the account of Genesis 3, it is fresh to me. I suppose I'm like most people, knowing that judgment came upon the man and woman after they succumbed to the serpent's temptation. But that's not the first thing that happened—God first promised that the Savior would come, proving for all time that "mercy triumphs over judgment" (James 2:13 NIV). This promise came as God condemned the serpent, saying, "I will put enmity between thee and the woman, and between thy seed and her seed; it shall bruise thy head, and thou shalt bruise his heel" (Genesis 3:15).

Within these words are found all the truths that make up the gospel of Christ. At first glance this is hard to see, but remember that an oak lies within an acorn. Likewise, the grand mystery of incarnation is found here—Christ is the seed of the woman. This promised seed was all that Adam had by way of revelation of God's purpose. Surely he passed this hope on to his sons, and Abel believed. By this light, Abel brought the firstborn of his flock and laid them on an altar, and his murder proved that the seed of the serpent hated the seed of the woman.

THE GRAND MYSTERY OF INCARNATION IS FOUND HERE.

Thereafter every generation of believers died without receiving the promised salvation, though they saw it from a distance. Is it too much to expect that our generation would daily thank God that *unto us* was born the Savior who is Christ the Lord?

NIGHT

I will put enmity between thee and the woman, and between thy seed and her seed; it shall bruise thy head, and thou shalt bruise his heel" (Genesis 3:15). At first glance this text about the two seeds looks difficult, and it is like a hard seed out of which grows grace and truth: "A virgin shall conceive, and bear a son, and shall call his name Immanuel" (Isaiah 7:14).

The two seeds are seen in Cain and Abel, Isaac and Ishmael, Jacob and Esau, even David and Goliath. So we are informed, "But as then he that was born after the flesh persecuted him that was born after the Spirit, even so it is now" (Galatians 4:29). The hostility between these two seeds has found its way into your own heart where "the sinful nature desires what is contrary to the Spirit, and the Spirit what is contrary to the sinful nature. They are in conflict with each other, so that you do not do what you want" (Galatians 5:17 NIV).

God advised the serpent of the coming seed of the woman, saying "It shall bruise thy head." This foretells the accomplishment of all things— the breaking of Satan's power and the cleansing of sin in Christ's death, the destruction of death by resurrection, the liberation of captivity in the ascension, and the victory of truth through the descent of the Spirit. It gives hope for the day in which Satan will be bound and when the evil one is cast into the lake of fire. These few words, "It shall bruise thy head," tell not only of the conflict but also of the *conquest*. They may not have been fully understood by those who first heard them, but to us, for whom the mystery is revealed, they are full of light.

Adam gave names to all the animals, but when

God presented the woman, she was not given a name. Soon the couple failed and fell and then heard the good news: They would not die, as they no doubt supposed (Genesis 2:17). There would be a seed of the woman! Though he was cursed, Adam immediately turned to the woman and called her Eve, "because she was the mother of all living" (Genesis 3:20).

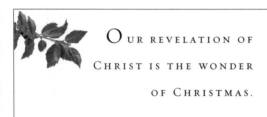

OUR REVELATION OF CHRIST IS THE WONDER OF CHRISTMAS.

Our revelation of Christ as compared to that of Adam is like the brightness of the sun to a tiny star, and it is the wonder of Christmas. We see that the baby in the manger grew up to be our Redeemer—the seed of the woman came! "O the depth of the riches both of the wisdom and knowledge of God! how unsearchable are his judgments, and his ways past finding out!" (Romans 11:33).

ABOUT THE AUTHOR

Daniel Partner, a veteran Christian author and editor, lives in Coos Bay, Oregon. His books include *I Give Myself to Prayer*, *All Things Are Possible*, *Peace Like a River*, *Women of Sacred Song* (written with his wife Margaret), and *The One-Year Book of Poetry* (coedited with Philip Comfort). All are available at Christian bookstores nationwide.

Besides his publishing work, Daniel is active in preserving and performing mid-nineteenth-century American popular music. Contact him by e-mail at author@danpartner.com.

If you enjoyed

THE
WONDER OF
CHRISTMAS

be sure to check out this title. . .
also available from Barbour Publishing: